Advanced Dungeons & Dragons 2nd Edition

Player's Handbook

Rules Supplement

The Complete
Bard's
Handbook

by Blake Mobley

TSR Inc.

Table of Contents

TSR, Inc.
POB 756
Lake Geneva,
WI 53147
U.S.A.

TSR Ltd.
120 Church End,
Cherry Hinton
Cambridge CB1 3LB
United Kingdom

2127

CREDITS
Design: Blake Mobley
Design Resource: Tim Beach
Editing: Mike Breault
Black and White Art: Terry Dykstra, Valerie Valusek
Color Art: Carol Heyer, John and Laura Lakey, Glen Orbik,
  Clyde Caldwell
Typography: Angelika Lokotz
Production: Paul Hanchette

In every era and every region throughout the world, traveling musicians wandered throughout the land. They moved from town to town, making a living by plying their trade as artists of sound and motion. In the AD&D® game, adventurers who do this are called *bards*.

Historically, bards were the poet-musicians of the Celtic peoples living in the British Isles (the Irish, Welsh, and Scots). Bards composed music, sang songs, and entertained their masters. Usually they worked for noblemen and spent their time honoring these noblemen and their families in song and music. Bards often accompanied their songs on the *crwth*, a type of lyre. Since their music wasn't written down, most of it has vanished.

During the early Middle Ages, bards had considerable political power and influence in the royal houses. However, in 1284 A.D., Edward I conquered Wales; the resulting turmoil reduced the importance of bards. Noblemen had more pressing concerns, and bards were left to fend for themselves. A few lingered on, into the 17th and 18th centuries in Ireland and Scotland as folk singers and musicians, but they eventually vanished along with their music.

During the 19th century, a determined effort was made to revive the bardic tradition. Folk music gatherings took place in and near Wales. These neo-bardic activities caught on among the public, and today the annual Eisteddfod folk festival is a popular and growing event in this region of the world.

Thus, bards have shown a cunning knack to survive through the ages. In one form or another, bards have been around for nearly 1,000 years. Besides the Eisteddfod festival, the bard has been immortalized in the genre of fantasy. Now you have a chance to continue the bardic tradition. This book covers not only the traditional bard, but expands the class with new and unique character kits. All of these kits involve some form of live entertainment, as all bards are entertainers at heart.

Nearly half of these kits entertain through music in one form or another: poetry, song, instruments, etc. But some present such diverse new kits as the Blade, who entertains through creative weapon displays, knife throwing, and sword swallowing. Read on and enjoy.

Optional Rules

Within this book are many new rules, bard kits, suggestions on role-playing, details of instruments, and new proficiencies. This information adds to the rules presented in the *Player's Handbook*.

It is important to note that this book is a supplement to the *Player's Handbook*. All of the rules presented here are optional. As a player, you must have your Dungeon Master's consent before using any of these new rules.

The Complete Bard's Handbook is a book of supplemental rules for adding depth, spice, and life to the bard character class. However, even if your Dungeon Master should decide that none of the rules within this book can used in his campaign, you can still gain a lot by reading the pages that follow. Most of the important tables from the *Player's Handbook* (*e.g.*, level advancement, bard abilities, etc.) are compressed into one convenient section within this book. It is also possible to mimic most of the new bard kits within the existing bard class. This book answers many questions about bardic abilities and presents an extensive list of instruments available to medieval bards, along with illustrations. And, finally, this book has a lot of good information to help gamers to better role-play their bard characters.

The Other Complete Books

The Complete Bard's Handbook is the sixth book of the PHBR series. If you find this book useful in your gaming, you may want to look into the other PHBRs.

Table 1: THE COMPLETE PHBR LINE

Designator	Topic	Stock #
PHBR1	Fighter's	2110
PHBR2	Thief's	2111
PHBR3	Priest's	2113
PHBR4	Wizard's	2115
PHBR5	Psionics	2117
PHBR6	Bard's	2127

All of these books contain much information that can enhance your bard. Some of the more useful information is listed below.

The Complete Fighter's Handbook: The "Character Creation" section provides an indepth look into the armorer proficiency. Those bard kits able to wear non-standard armor will find this topic particularly interesting. Weapon quality and its effects on combat are also discussed. The "Role-Playing" section provides a list of warrior personalities, some of which could be adopted by bard characters. Since some bards are adept with numerous weapons, the section on combat rules applies to certain bards (particularly the expanded weapon proficiency rules, which allow a character to learn multiple weapons while expending only a few proficiency slots). Fighting styles, martial arts, and other odd combat rules are also presented here. Even jousting tournaments are covered (ideal for the Gallant kit). Within the "Equipment" section is a sizable collection of new weapons, new armor, and new magical items.

The Complete Thief's Handbook: As you might expect, this handbook has a great deal of useful information for the bard class. Within are more useful rules than can be listed here. However, general topics you may find helpful include the following: role-playing thieves, new proficiencies, guilds (construction, maintenance, and types), thief tools, thief equipment, new magical items, classic cons (especially good for the Charlatan), new thief rules, and a description of the thief-based campaign.

The Complete Priest's Handbook: There is little information in this handbook that is pertinent to the bard character class.

The Complete Wizard's Handbook: Chapter 4 discusses campaign worlds with varying levels of magic. Chapter 5 covers wizards and combat. Chapter 6 describes spell casting under water, spell functioning on various planes, and impaired casting. Chapter 7 presents a commentary on new applications for old spells, adjudicating illusions, spell research, and magical item research. Chapter 8 gives all-new spells ranging from 1st to 8th level. Finally, Chapter 9 contains a number of useful wizardly lists.

The Complete Psionics Handbook: There are two useful elements within this book. Most important are the wild talents in Chapter 1. It is possible for a bard to have a few wild psionic talents (the process for determining this is given in Chapter 1). If a wild talent

is discovered, the bard player will find the rest of this book invaluable, as it contains all the information needed to run a psionically endowed bard. Also, note that all player character Gypsy-bards are wild talents. The psionics book also contains a number of challenging psionic monsters.

How to Use This Handbook

How players use this handbook depends upon their skill level, seriousness about the bard character class, and their relationship with their Dungeon Master.

Skilled players who are serious about role-playing bard characters will want to read this book closely. Those who are not as serious will find the table of contents (in the front of this book) and the index (in the back) to be invaluable in locating topics of interest.

A new bard character record sheet is located at the back of this handbook. It has been custom-tailored to the bard character class. You will find spaces to place every detail of your bard. Furthermore, the sheet has been laid out with numerous helpful notes, comments, and formats to provide you with a plethora of information without referring to the rule books. You may photocopy the sheet for your own personal use.

For those of you who wish to create new bard kits, a handy kit creation sheet is also bound into the back of this book. This may also be photocopied for personal use.

It is not necessary for you to read this book from cover to cover unless you wish to be the ultimate bard role-player. Instead, locate the section you wish to explore in greater detail and read it to your own satisfaction.

A major effort has been made to make this handbook complete, as its title states. Many of the rules specific to bards in both the *Player's Handbook* and *Dungeon Master's Guide* have been complied and condensed within this handbook. Also contained herein is the information needed to generate a bard and maintain him during level advancements. The commonly asked questions about standard bards have been attended to, along with rules clarifications where needed. The bard class has also been fully defined for all to see. The fine points of the class have been examined, illuminated, and made more accessible. Finally, there are many added details concerning role-playing, including the bard personality, reputation, and role as a performer.

Now it is time to begin creating your own bard player character. Before you decide whether he is flippant and cavalier or stately and pondering, whether he is skilled at playing the lyre and reciting lyrics or spinning tales of long-lost heroes, first you must generate and record his fundamental character statistics.

This section includes the basic information needed to generate a bard. The following information is a comprehensive summary of the Rogue and Bard sections found in the *Player's Handbook*. It is assumed that any player using this book is intimately familiar with the *Player's Handbook*; thus, space is not spent here upon background and role-playing information. For a general discussion of these topics, refer to the Rogue and Bard sections found in Chapter 3 of the *Player's Handbook*. Of course, *The Complete Bard's Handbook* would hardly be complete without discussing such subjects. Refer to the "Role-Playing Bards" section of this book for a detailed examination of these topics.

Qualifications

Generating ability scores high enough to qualify for the bard class is difficult. In fact, it is unlikely unless your DM allows one of the alternative dice-rolling methods described in Chapter 1 of the *Player's Handbook*. A complete discussion on generating bard player characters (along with pre-generated bards) using all six dice-rolling methods is presented at the end of this section.

To be a bard or not to be a bard, these are the qualifications (see Table 2).

Table 2: CLASS QUALIFICATIONS

Ability Requirements:
Dexterity 12
Intelligence 13
Charisma 15

Prime Requisites*: Dexterity, Charisma
Races Allowed: Human, Half-elf
Alignments Allowed: Any Neutral
   (LN, NG, N, NE, CN)

*Bards with a 16 or better in both Dexterity and Charisma gain a 10% bonus to their awarded experience points.

Core Abilities

Bards can wear any armor providing Armor Class 5 (chain mail) or worse. Other forms of armor are simply too constraining, heavy, and awkward for true entertainers to wear. Likewise, bards cannot employ shields, as these get in the way of activities such as playing instruments or performing sleight-of-hand tricks. Carrying a lute around in the dungeon is hard enough without worrying about a large metal shield banging around and getting in the way.

Table 3: ARMOR ALLOWED

Armor	AC	Cost (gp)	Weight (lb)
Leather Armor	8	5	15
Padded Armor	8	4	10
Studded Leather	7	20	25
Ring Mail	7	100	30
Hide Armor	6	15	30
Brigandine Armor	6	120	35
Scale Mail	6	120	40
Chain Mail	5	75	40

Although bards fight as rogues and calculate their THAC0s accordingly, they are allowed to use any weapon. Cost, weight, damage, and other relevant statistics for all weapons are found in Chapter 6 of the *Player's Handbook*.

All rogues (including bards) use Table 25 of the *Player's Handbook* to determine level and hit dice based upon experience points. As noted in the expanded reprint of this table be-

low, a six-sided die is used to determine hit point increases for bards of level 1 through 10 (plus any Constitution adjustments).

After 10th level, bards gain 2 hit points per level advanced. A hit die is no longer rolled and Constitution adjustments no longer apply.

Table 4: EXPERIENCE LEVELS

Level	XP Needed	Hit Dice (d6)	THAC0
1	0	1	20
2	1,250	2	20
3	2,500	3	19
4	5,000	4	19
5	10,000	5	18
6	20,000	6	18
7	40,000	7	17
8	70,000	8	17
9	110,000	9	16
10	160,000	10	16
11	220,000	10 + 2	15
12	440,000	10 + 4	15
13	660,000	10 + 6	14
14	880,000	10 + 8	14
15	1,100,000	10 + 10	13
16	1,320,000	10 + 12	13
17	1,540,000	10 + 14	12
18	1,760,000	10 + 16	12
19	1,980,000	10 + 18	11
20	2,200,000	10 + 20	11

Proficiency and saving throw numbers are listed in the following table to complete the information for level advancement. If a bard uses a weapon with which he isn't proficient, a −3 attack roll penalty is incurred.

Table 5: LEVEL IMPROVEMENTS

Level	Prof. W	N/W	Saving Throws PPDM	RSW	PP	BW	S
1	2	3	13	14	12	16	15
2	2	3	13	14	12	16	15
3	2	3	13	14	12	16	15
4	3	4	13	14	12	16	15
5	3	4	12	12	11	15	13
6	3	4	12	12	11	15	13
7	3	4	12	12	11	15	13
8	4	5	12	12	11	15	13
9	4	5	11	10	10	14	11
10	4	5	11	10	10	14	11
11	4	5	11	10	10	14	11
12	5	6	11	10	10	14	11
13	5	6	10	8	9	13	9
14	5	6	10	8	9	13	9
15	5	6	10	8	9	13	9
16	6	7	10	8	9	13	9
17	6	7	9	6	8	12	7
18	6	7	9	6	8	12	7
19	6	7	9	6	8	12	7
20	7	8	9	6	8	12	7
21	7	8	8	4	4	11	5

Proficiency Abbreviations:
  W: Weapon Proficiency slots
  N/W: Nonweapon Proficiency slots

Saving Throw Abbreviations:
  PPDM: Paralyzation, Poison, or Death Magic
  RSW: Rod, Staff, or Wand
  PP: Petrification or Polymorph
  BW: Breath Weapon
  S: Spell

In addition to their many special abilities, bards dabble in wizardry. They gain no spells until 2nd level and they progress through the spell levels slower than true wizards. However, they are very adept learners, so their casting level is equal to their experience level. Thus, although a bard gains his first spell at 2nd level, he casts that spell as a 2nd-level spellcaster. For example, if the 2nd-level bard

memorized *affect normal fires*, it would last for four rounds when cast (two rounds/level).

Table 6: SPELL PROGRESSION

Bard Level	Spell Level					
	1	2	3	4	5	6
1	—	—	—	—	—	—
2	1	—	—	—	—	—
3	2	—	—	—	—	—
4	2	1	—	—	—	—
5	3	1	—	—	—	—
6	3	2	—	—	—	—
7	3	2	1	—	—	—
8	3	3	1	—	—	—
9	3	3	2	—	—	—
10	3	3	2	1	—	—
11	3	3	3	1	—	—
12	3	3	3	2	—	—
13	3	3	3	2	1	—
14	3	3	3	3	1	—
15	3	3	3	3	2	—
16	4	3	3	3	2	1
17	4	4	3	3	3	1
18	4	4	4	3	3	2
19	4	4	4	4	3	2
20	4	4	4	4	4	3

Besides just dabbling in wizardry, 10th-level bards have the powerful ability to use any written magical item, whether it is a scroll, book, map, or other written form. This skill is not limited by normal class restrictions. Thus, bards can use clerical scrolls, wizard scrolls, and even magical books restricted to other classes.

Since all bards are dabblers and not devotees of the magical arts, their understanding of written magic is imperfect. There is a 15% chance that they use the work incorrectly. The consequences of incorrect use is up to the DM, but they are almost certain to be unpleasant. (It is common for a bard's allies to flee in panic when he begins to read such items.)

Bards are most renowned for their communication and entertainment talents. To en-hance these skills, they pick up a number of thief skills. Of course, when times are lean, many bards ply these abilities in less-than-honorable manners.

All four of these skills are treated as the equivalent thief skills. Skill bases are listed below.

Table 7: BASE THIEF ABILITIES

Pick Pockets	Detect Noise	Climb Walls	Read Languages
10%	20%	50%	5%

The player also gets 20 points to distribute among the four skills at 1st level and 15 additional points every time the bard advances in level. If these points are distributed so as to gradually equalize the skills, the bard might advance each level as indicated on Table 8.

Table 8: BARD AVERAGE THIEF SKILLS

Level	Pick Pockets	Detect Noise	Climb Walls	Read Lang.
1	16	25	53	11
2	20	28	56	16
3	24	33	58	20
4	29	36	60	25
5	33	40	63	29
6	37	44	65	34
7	41	48	68	38
8	46	52	70	42
9	50	56	72	47
10	54	59	75	52
11	59	63	77	56
12	63	67	79	61
13	67	71	82	65
14	71	75	84	70
15	76	78	87	74
16	80	82	89	79
17	84	86	91	84
18	88	90	94	88
19	93	94	95	93
20	95	95	95	95

As with all rogues, a bard's thief abilities are adjusted by race, Dexterity, and armor worn.

Table 9: THIEF SKILL ADJUSTMENTS

Race	Pick Pockets	Detect Noise	Climb Walls	Read Lang.
Human	—	—	—	—
Half-elf	+10%	—	—	—
Dwarf	—	—	−10%	5%
Elf	+5%	+5%	—	—
Gnome	—	+5%	—	—
Halfling	+5%	+5%	−15%	−5%

Dexterity Adjustments

Dex	Pick Pockets	Detect Noise	Climb Walls	Read Lang.
9	−15%	—	—	—
10	−10%	—	—	—
11	−5%	—	—	—
12	—	—	—	—
13-15	—	—	—	—
16	—	—	—	—
17	+5%	—	—	—
18	+10%	—	—	—
19	+15%	—	—	—

Kit Adjustments

Kit	Pick Pockets	Detect Noise	Climb Walls	Read Lang.
True Bard	—	—	—	—
Blade	—	+5%	+5%	−5%
Charlatan	+5%	—	—	+5%
Gallant	−25%	—	−5%	+5%
Gypsy	+10%	+5%	−10%	−5%
Herald	−5%	+10%	−10%	+5%
Jester	+10%	−5%	—	−10%
Jongleur	+5%	—	+15%	−5%
Loremaster	−5%	+5%	−10%	+15%
Meistersinger	−10%	+10%	—	−10%
Riddlemaster	—	+5%	+5%	+5%
Skald	—	+5%	—	−25%
Thespian	+5%	+5%	—	+5%

Demi-Bards

Demi-Bard	Pick Pockets	Detect Noise	Climb Walls	Read Lang.
Dwarf Chanter	−5%	—	+5%	—
Elf Minstrel	—	—	—	—
Gnome Prof.	−5%	—	—	+10%
Half. Whistler	—	+10%	—	—

Armor

Type of Armor	Pick Pockets	Detect Noise	Climb Walls	Read Lang.
None*	+5%	—	+10%	—
Leather	—	—	—	—
Padded	−30%	−10%	−30%	—
Studded Leath.	−30%	−10%	−30%	—
Ring Mail	−25%	−10%	−25%	—
Brigandine	−20%	−10%	−25%	—
Scale Mail	−25%	−15%	−40%	—
Hide Armor	−30%	−5%	−30%	—
Chain Mail	−25%	−10%	−25%	—
Elven Chain	−20%	−5%	−20%	—

*Includes small magical items, such as rings, bracers, and cloaks, but not large or bulky devices.

If you compare these armor adjustments to the "Effects of Armor on Thief Skills" table in *The Complete Thief's Handbook*, you see that bards have a special advantage when using ring mail, brigandine, scale mail, hide armor, and chain mail. Since bards often wear such armor while thieves do not, bards are more comfortable and familiar with the workings of these armor types. Thus, bards suffer only about half the skill penalties that thieves suffer if wearing the same armor.

If your DM allows a bard to put on any form of armor normally disallowed to the class (as suggested by certain kits, for purposes of disguise, out of necessity, or for the sake of entertainment), the penalties are identical to those for a thief in similar armor.

Table 10: ILLEGAL ARMOR ADJUSTMENT

Armor Type	Pick Pockets	Hear Noise	Climb Walls	Read Lang.
Splint Mail	−40%	−25%	−50%	—
Banded Armor	−50%	−30%	−90%	—
Plate Mail	−75%	−50%	−95%	—
Bronze Plate	−75%	−50%	−95%	—
Field Plate	−95%	−70%	−95%	—
Full Plate	−95%	−70%	−95%	—

At 9th level, bards attract 10d6 0-level followers who arrive as soon as the bard secures a stronghold.

The above information defines the standard bard character class. This core is common to all bards no matter what setting, history, personality, or bard kit is used. As such, it does not include the special kit abilities or personality aspects that make a character stand out. This type of information is found in the chapter on character kits later in this book.

The experienced player will note that many of the bard's special abilities listed in the *Player's Handbook* are missing in the above treatment. That is because the standard bard, as detailed in the *Player's Handbook*, is considered a complete kit unto itself. It is called the True Bard kit. This kit combines the core information above with the kit approach of this book to define the bard as it appears in the *Player's Handbook*.

Generating Ability Scores

Chapter 1 of the *Player's Handbook* presents six die rolling methods for generating player characters. Ability scores have been pre-generated below that qualify for the bard using all six of these methods. The probability of generating a qualifying bard with each method is also provided. Note that it is very difficult to generate a bard by the standard method (method I). Only by using one of the alternative methods do you have a good chance to roll up a bard.

If these alternative methods are used, method VI will practically guarantee a qualifying character. Methods IV and V are also likely to succeed. Although methods II and III are less likely to result in a qualifying bard, they are still better than method I. However, if your DM does not allow for these alternative methods, do not badger him. After all, it is his right to select the rules used in his campaign. This will make the bard much more special when a qualifying character is finally rolled.

Table 11:
PREGENERATED ABILITY SCORES

Method I (under 1%)

Sample Bard #	Str	Dex	Con	Int	Wis	Cha
1	10	13	11	13	10	15
2	11	13	14	13	14	16
3	9	13	15	13	8	16
4	7	12	6	16	11	15
5	12	14	8	13	6	17
6	11	12	11	13	7	16

Method II (almost 5%)

Sample Bard #	Str	Dex	Con	Int	Wis	Cha
1	12	15	14	16	13	16
2	10	13	13	15	16	15
3	9	12	13	13	12	15
4	15	12	14	13	14	15
5	14	12	12	13	11	16
6	9	16	17	14	14	15

Method III (slightly over 29%)

Sample Bard #	3d6 Rolls					
1	17,	13,	13,	10,	9,	8
2	15,	14,	13,	11,	8,	6
3	17,	16,	12,	11,	9,	6
4	16,	14,	14,	13,	12,	11
5	18,	15,	13,	13,	11,	11
6	16,	13,	13,	10,	8,	7

Method IV (slightly under 66%)

Sample Bard #	Six Best 3d6 Rolls					
1	15,	14,	14,	13,	11,	11
2	18,	16,	14,	14,	13,	12
3	15,	14,	14,	13,	11,	11
4	15,	15,	13,	13,	13,	11
5	15,	15,	14,	13,	12,	11
6	15,	14,	13,	13,	13,	11

Method V (slightly under 75%)

Sample Bard #	4d6 Rolls, Drop Low d6					
1	17,	15,	14,	12,	10,	9
2	17,	16,	13,	13,	11,	10
3	18,	15,	13,	13,	12,	10
4	16,	15,	13,	12,	12,	10
5	15,	14,	13,	11,	10,	9
6	15,	14,	12,	11,	11,	6

Method VI (slightly under 98%)

Sample Bard #	8 Pts Per Ability, Add 7d6 As Desired					
1	16	14	12	11	9	9
2	17	14	13	11	10	8
3	18	13	13	12	10	9
4	17	15	13	13	11	10
5	15	14	12	12	9	8
6	16	13	12	11	11	9

All of the above statistics qualify for a bard player character. If it is agreeable to you and your Dungeon Master, you may simply roll 1d6 and consult any of the above tables your DM allows for a quick way to generate your bard's ability scores. If your DM allows all six methods, you can even roll a first d6 to select the table, then a second d6 to select the actual ability scores.

Method I and II require ability scores to be recorded in the order rolled. This has been done for you. Since methods III and up allow the player to assign the scores as desired, these scores have been organized from high to low for your convenience. Method VI is unusual. Every ability starts with a base score of 8. The player then rolls 7d6 and adds the results to the base 8 in any order or combination. However, the full count of a die must be added entirely to one ability. If this causes the ability to raise above 18, then the die cannot be used on that ability.

Kits can be thought of as subclasses of the bard character class. They all represent bard characters, but each is unique enough to warrant individual treatment by those players who enjoy examining the finer points of the bard class.

All of the bard kits are set up the same way. There are ten possible subsections to each kit that flesh out the kit and delineate its unique aspects. The details of these subsections are described below.

If the word "Standard" is listed under any subsection, it means that the information that would normally go in that section is identical to the standard information for the True Bard. Actually, every kit's subsections should be thought of as having the "Standard" default. If any question ever arises as to the limits or extensions of a kit, the True Bard kit should be consulted.

Kit Subsections

Specialty: That kit's entertainment form.

Qualifications: Qualifications will limit or extend allowed race, alignment, and ability scores for the particular kit.

Introduction: This section presents a colorful, first-person example of the kit. Listen to the NPC as he chats with you about himself and his kind.

Description: This section describes the kit and distinguishes this particular type of bard from the others.

Role: Role explains the role that this type of bard plays within a party and in society as a whole.

Secondary Skills: Secondary skills is an optional rule found in Chapter 5 of the *Player's Handbook*. If this rule is used, only skills listed in this subsection of the kit can be selected by characters who adopt this kit.

Weapon Proficiencies: A character can become proficient only in the weapons listed in this subsection.

Nonweapon Proficiencies: Although non-

weapon proficiencies are an optional rule, it is strongly recommended that they be used if bard kits are allowed into the game. They have been carefully selected to give each kit a unique feel.

Bonuses: Each bard kit has four bonus proficiencies. These proficiencies are gained without expending any proficiency slots. It is strongly suggested that at least half of a bard's proficiency slots be spent in one of three ways: gaining proficiencies from among those on the "Suggested" list, gaining additional topics (see the chapter on proficiencies) to proficiencies on the Bonus or Suggested lists, or in improving proficiencies on either list.

Armor/Equipment: Armor restrictions or extensions are listed here. Sometimes special comments will be made about equipment, such as typical dress, identifying colors, special tools, and so on.

Special Benefits: Each bard kit has four special benefits. These benefits set the kit off from all other character classes and kits. The character should take on a different role-playing feel because of the kit's descriptive information.

Special Hindrances: Special hindrances or limitations are placed on certain kits. Hindrances are listed here only if they do not fall into any subsection listed earlier.

Notes: On rare occasions, this subsection is used to list special notes that don't fit into any of the earlier subsections.

List of Kits

All of the bard kits are listed on the following pages. The first kit is that of the True Bard, as presented in the *Player's Handbook*. This kit establishes a base from which all the other kits are built. The other kits are arranged in alphabetical order. A section on multi-classed bards follows. It contains an additional four kits, but these are restricted to demihumans.

True Bard

Specialty: Jack-of-all-trades.

Qualifications: Standard ability scores (Dexterity of 12, Intelligence of 13, and Charisma of 15).

Introduction: This is a typical bard right out of the *Player's Handbook*. No introductions are needed.

Description: Bards are described in the *Player's Handbook*. They are the epitome of the jack-of-all-trades, able to wield all weapons, don most types of armor, cast a good number of wizard spells, and employ four of the eight thief skills. Bards are very versatile, but they are masters of no craft.

As with all bards, True Bards are entertainers. They can sing, play instruments, create and recite poetry, and spin tall tales. In fact, a bard's skill at these art forms is such that he can inspire and rally allies and even negate the effects of hostile songs and sounds.

Bards are always able to read and write their native language. They know much about local history, and they can relate legends pertaining to many of the powerful magical items they encounter in their travels.

Bards are tremendous listeners, readers, and searchers. They eagerly listen to any news and stories that folk are willing to tell. If there's anything available for a bard to learn, he'll learn it as soon as he can.

Role: Bards are excellent characters to play in small gaming groups. Their varied skills enable them to fill in for many more-specialized characters. For example, a bard could serve as a small group's wizard and thief. They are great survivalists, as they can almost always find some skill to help them out of any predicament they fall into.

Secondary Skills: True Bards may select any secondary skill.

Weapon Proficiencies: Bards are unrestricted as to weaponry, but they rarely carry around bulky weapons, even if they are proficient with them. A bard seen carrying a two-handed sword or halberd is likely to arouse suspicions about his intentions. A bard with an elegant bow across his back, however, does not draw as much attention. A finely crafted weapon even adds a touch of class to the bard's appearance.

Nonweapon Proficiencies: *Bonuses:* Singing, Musical Instrument, Reading/Writing (native tongue), Local History.

Other proficiencies may be selected as desired. For every additional proficiency slot spent in the musical instrument proficiency, bards not only increase their ability, but they also gain the use of two more instruments. A bard initially knows how to play one instrument (of the player's choosing). If a second proficiency slot is used for musical instruments, the bard can now accompany himself on three instruments.

Armor/Equipment: The bard can use any weapon. He can wear any armor up to, and including, chain mail, but he cannot use a shield. True Bards generally wear bright, cheerful colors, sometimes wearing plumed hats to complete the ensemble. Their instruments, clothing, and other equipment are all kept in top condition.

Special Benefits: *Influence Reactions:* When performing for an audience, the bard can attempt to alter the mood of his listeners. Such an audience must not be attacking or preparing for an immediate attack. The bard must be singing, chanting, spinning a tale, reciting a powerful oratory, or playing a tune on an instrument with which he is proficient. The intended effect of the performance is determined by the bard's player; he may want to make the audience friendlier or more hostile, for instance. After a length of time (1d10 rounds is suggested), all NPCs able to hear the performance (regardless of whether or not they are paying attention) must roll a saving throw vs. paralyzation. For small groups, roll individual saving throws. For large groups, the DM may split the audience into groups of ten or so and roll a separate saving throw for each

group. There is a −1 penalty to the saving throw for every three levels of experience of the bard. Those failing the roll have their reactions adjusted one level (from friendly to indifferent, for example) in the desired direction—consult Table 59: Encounter Reactions, in the *DMG*. Those whose saving throws succeed have their reactions adjusted one level in the direction opposite from that intended by the bard.

Rally Allies: To use this ability, the bard must know the nature of the upcoming combat. A bard can't rally allies if there is no obvious opponent. Rallying allies is done is much the same manner as influencing reactions. The bard sings heroic songs or weaves inspiring tales about how his comrades will overcome their foes and win the day. Such heroic recitals always take at least three rounds, and the audience must be in close proximity to the bard for the effects to occur (within a 10-foot radius per level of the bard). When complete, all the affected allies automatically receive one of the following three benefits (as decided by the bard's player): +1 to attack rolls, +1 to saving throws, or +2 to morale. The chosen effect lasts one round per level of the bard. The effects can be renewed by the bard, even during the same encounter, but combatants have to return to within the bard's radius and listen to his tales for another three rounds. It is impossible to rally allies who are actively battling opponents.

Note that the benefit applies only to the specific encounter that the bard sings about. It does not apply to a ranger who hears the tale, rides off on his horse to warn the rear guard, and is then ambushed by wandering bandits.

Counter Song: Another powerful use of story, song, or tale when voiced by a bard is that of counter song. This is the intricate art of canceling the effects of hostile sound, whether it be songs, chants, wails, or even commands and suggestions from magical spells. In order to sing the proper counter song or chant the proper counter poem, a bard must concen-

trate intensely. He may perform no additional actions other than a slow (half speed) walk. If he is struck by an attack or fails a saving throw, his attempt is ruined. The exertion is such that only one counter song may be attempted per encounter or battle.

Success of the counter song is realized only if the bard rolls a successful saving throw vs. spell. If this is successful, the hostile sounds have no effects within 30 feet of the bard. If the saving throw fails, the bard's attempt is fruitless and the hostile sounds have their standard effects (applicable saving throws and other defenses still apply).

Counter singing does not prevent hostile spellcasters from reading scrolls, using magical item command words, or casting spells (even spells with verbal components). Counter singing does prevent all other hostile sounds from functioning, including spell effects that require the caster to speak (*e.g., command, quest, suggestion, tongues, etc.*).

Legend Lore: One of the most useful abilities of the bard is his knowledge of famous magical items and uncanny knack for figuring out how they function. To perform legend lore, the bard must scrutinize the item closely. This does not necessarily require actually handling the item, but it must be fully visible to the bard.

Scrutiny takes 1d10 rounds, after which a percentile roll is made. The bard has a 5% chance per level of knowing something about the item. The exact information revealed is up to the DM. The bard draws upon history, rumors, and clues based on the item's construction to gain this information. Typical information revealed includes the item's history, maker, name, and other less technical aspects. Information such as the number of pluses, exact command words, etc., are rarely learned. This type of specific information is left for spells, such as *identify, commune, limited wish*, and so on.

A good optional rule is to give some very specific information to the bard player if the

roll is equal to or less than the bard's level. Furthermore, if the roll is 01, the bard should know almost everything there is to know about the item.

If the DM allows it, the following table may be used as a fast optional method to determine what is known about an item that was successfully examined by a bard. To use this table, the bard must first succeed with the legend lore percentile roll. If this roll succeeds, the player should roll on the following table once per level of the bard. Results that come up more than once are not rerolled; the bard simply knows a lot about this aspect of the item. After rolling, give the DM some time to come up with a suitable background and history. Few items are detailed with this type of information. After all, bards tend to be more curious about the legends and lore that lie behind an item's powers than most others.

Table 12: LEGEND LORE RESULTS

3d6 Roll	Information Gained
3	How many charges/uses left
4	Whether item is intelligent
5	Whether items is cursed/evil
6	Value on the open market
7	Name
8	Famous past owners
9	Age of item
10	What race created it
11	Where it was made
12	Who crafted it
13	Alignment of owners
14	Who can use it
15	General effects
16	How to activate it
17	Item type (as per *DMG*)
18	Let player read *DMG* entry

Special Hindrances: None.

Blade

Specialty: Assassin/Spy/Weapon Master.

Qualifications: Blades must have a Dexterity of 13 or more, an Intelligence of at least 13, and a Charisma of 15 or more.

Introduction: *So you want to know about Blades, eh? Well, keep out of the way and I can show you about myself and those like me. My name's Dark and I'm a Blade. I take my name from the black garb that I wear at all times. I'm actually not exceptional in this, as all Blades dress in dark clothing. But the name has stuck, and I like it.*

I currently work for a small carnival that travels around the mid-Flanaess, entertaining the local crowds and thrilling the women. My tricks are similar to those of most Blades. I perform sword dances, swallow sabers, put on weapon displays, and perform feats of knife throwing. Most crowds are especially enthralled when I strap Tatanna, a young-looking elf maiden, to a wooden plank, blindfold myself, step back 12 paces, then encircle her body in a wall of knives.

Entertaining fools is only my surface career. On the last day of a performance, a half dozen of my fellow performers and I stage the real entertainment—at least from my point of view. We slip into the upper class section of town and relieve some pompous wealthy dupe of his family fortune.

Although these "side shows" are very profitable, they still don't give me the old thrill that I used to get. Thus, I've turned to a more daring hobby—assassination. I'm not a "Blade for hire," and I absolutely hate those mindless, ruthless killers. What I do is feel out a town to discover who's oppressing the populace the most. Once I've found the biggest bully in town, I slip into his residence, spy on him, and plan his untimely demise. Then I perform my greatest solo act. I slip into the fellow's bedroom, poison him, cast sound bubble, wake him, and then share in his last few moments of life.

Description: Blades are master artisans with bladed weapons. Everyone has seen a Blade in action at fairs and carnivals. They are the knife throwers who pop balloons while blindfolded and swallow slender sabers such as those used by lawless pirates on the high seas.

Blades also perform amazing displays of weapon skill and control as they flash various weapons all about their bodies with deadly precision. Oriental Blades are perhaps the most skilled at this particular art form. Using weapons such as the three-piece rod, nunchaku, or the katana, Oriental Blades put on amazing displays of rapid weapon movement, including offensive and defensive spins, katas, and ritual dances. Occidental Blades are also impressive, as they rapidly spin short swords, quarterstaves, or sickles about them.

Besides rapid displays of weapon skill, Blades also perform slow, elegant dances, involving incredibly precise movement and timing. These dances include thrusts, lunges, leaps, graceful arcs, etc.

If there is a showy way to wield, throw, or perform with a weapon, a Blade knows how to do it better than anyone.

Role: Blades have great reputations as the most deadly weapon masters in the land. This is generally far from the truth. Any warrior is more skilled than most Blades at successfully attacking opponents. Blades don't understand offensive and defensive weapon maneuvers, nor do they know the locations of vital body parts. Blades can be effective in many combat situations, however, as they use flash and flare to enhance their attacks.

Imagine what an orc would think if it was trapped in a cavern with only two exits and a man blocking each. One man (a warrior) wears plate mail and is calmly holding a long sword; the other (a Blade) is dressed in solid black studded leather armor and is grasping a

halberd. Both men advance upon the hapless orc, but the Blade begins rotating his halberd in an ever-quickening offensive spin, demonstrating masterful control of his weapon. Which opponent will the orc choose?

Blades are valuable aids to any party, as their amazing displays can have significant effects upon the resolve and morale of opponents.

For every Blade who leads an adventurous life, there is another who serves in the role of assassin. Blades make perfect killers, as they know how to climb walls, cast wizard spells, and use any weapon they choose. Furthermore, Blades can use their performing personae to gather information and even get themselves invited to perform within the homes of their victims.

Secondary Skills: Armorer, Bowyer/Fletcher, Gambler, Weaponsmith.

Weapon Proficiencies: At least half of a Blade's weapon proficiency slots must be selected from the following: sword (any), dagger, knife. Blades are also limited to expending but one slot on a purely missile weapon (one that cannot be used in melee combat). This does not include such weapons as spears or hand axes, which can be thrown or used in melee.

Nonweapon Proficiencies: *Bonuses:* Reading/Writing (native tongue), Local History, Blind-fighting, Juggling. *Suggested:* Blacksmithing, Bowyer/Fletcher, Disguise, Poetry, Weaponsmithing.

Armor/Equipment: To complement their entertainment image as mysterious and fearsome men, Blades often dress in black garb, even going so far as to wear masks, facial wraps, or black headgear. Their weapons are always kept in perfect condition and highly polished for maximum effect during a performance. A man dressed in solid black, flashing gleaming silver blades, is truly an awesome sight.

Special Benefits:

Weapons Display: For this ability to have an effect, the Blade must whirl a non-missile weapon about his body. The observer must be close enough to the Blade to see the display (*e.g.*, a *darkness* spell negates the effect). The display has no effect upon those already engaged in close combat, as they are too busy to pay attention to the show. Also, Weapons Display works only on those of Low (5) or better Intelligence, who can either use weapons or have seen them used. (It is impossible to impress green slime by twirling a dagger in your fingers.) Likewise, a highly intelligent creature that has never seen a weapon used will also be unintimidated by the Blade's display.

By whirling a melee or hurled weapon about, a Blade can affect the morale and courage of others. Such a display of skill, precision, and deadly grace lowers opponents' morale by 2 (but it does not require an immediate morale check) and inspires allies, giving a +1 bonus to allies' attack rolls.

The display must occur for a full round without interruption. During this time, any successful attack upon the Blade, or failed saving throw by the Blade, disrupts the display.

Weapons Display may be used only once per encounter; the display lasts for one round per level of the Blade.

This ability requires a lot of room; it cannot be done in a narrow corridor. Specifically, the Blade must be able to stand with his arms extended while holding out the weapon and be able to move his arms in all directions without contacting any obstructions.

Handle Weapon: Blades train and perform with weapons in both hands. Although all thieves are allowed to attack with two weapons (see Chapter 9 of the *PHB*), Blades suffer no penalty to their main weapon and only a −2 penalty to the attack roll with their secondary weapon.

Blades are considered to be ambidextrous. They can shoot a bow equally well with either their left or right hand, they can wield a sword

in either hand, and they can throw daggers with either hand—all with no penalties.

When a Blade tries to catch small weapons that are thrown at him, the attack roll (see the juggling proficiency) is made using the Blade's level as a bonus.

Trick Throw: Although this ability is called "trick throw," it functions the same for both missile weapons and hurled weapons. Trick throw enables a Blade to perform called shots (as per Chapter 9 in the *DMG*). The usual −4 attack roll penalty is lessened by 1 for every five experience levels of the Blade (round fractions up). Thus 1st- through 5th-level Blades suffer only a −3 penalty, 6th- through 10th-level Blades suffer only a −2 penalty, and so on.

Because Blades throw weapons blindfolded, they extend the blind-fighting proficiency to include hurled weapons and missile weapons (to a maximum range of 30 feet).

Defensive/Offensive Spin: Defensive and offensive spins are elements of a good weapon display. They have other uses as well.

A defensive spin is a specialized form of parrying (see Chapter 9 of the *PHB*) in which the Blade whirls his weapon to create a deadly shell about his body. A Blade may not attack during any round in which he is performing a defensive spin. The Blade's Armor Class is lowered by half the Blade's level (round fractions up) during this maneuver. In addition, any creature that makes a melee attack on the Blade must roll a successful saving throw vs. paralyzation or suffer damage equal to half the Blade's level (round fractions up; the damage is limited to the weapon's maximum damage, including any bonuses of the weapon). A defensive spin may be used only once per combat; it lasts for a maximum number of rounds equal to the Blade's Constitution. A successful hit upon the Blade disrupts his concentration and ends the defensive spin.

An offensive spin is a much more threatening maneuver. The Blade creates a fearsome-looking display of skill directed at a specific opponent. The spin must last for the entire round, during which the Blade does not attack (nor does he receive any Armor Class adjustment, as he would for a defensive spin). On the *next* round, the Blade makes a normal attack roll. If this hits, the victim must roll a successful morale check or it will try to stay at least ten feet from the Blade (going off to attack other members of the Blade's party or fleeing in terror if the Blade is the only available opponent). Offensive spins may be attempted only once on a particular creature. Furthermore, the Blade cannot have been damaged by that creature prior to the offensive spin attack (a creature won't fear someone it has already injured). This is a difficult condition to fulfill, as the creature gets a free round to attack while the Blade is the first round of the offensive spin. Offensive spins function only against creatures of Low (5) or better Intelligence.

If the Blade's spin is interrupted (either voluntarily or by a successful attack), the Blade does not get an attack that round.

Special Hindrances: Unlike many other bards, Blades do not gain the 10th-level ability to use all forms of written magical items. Blades study weapons, not scrolls, maps, and books.

Notes: Although Blades do not receive a single bonus to damage or attack rolls, and they fight as rogues, they are still some of the flashiest combatants you'll ever meet or play.

Charlatan

Specialty: Trickster/Con Artist.

Qualifications: Standard ability scores. Charlatans live off the fat of the land, bending all the rules and hopping through loopholes in the law. It is completely against the personality of the Charlatan to be lawful. Charlatans are limited to NG, N, NE, or CN alignments. Gnomes may become Charlatans and advance up to 6th level.

Introduction: *My real name is Tiel, but*

most of the fools who fall into my traps call me Tori. I know exactly how to get what I want from others. Especially those who are overconfident, weak, or emotional.

People often believe what they want to believe, and I take advantage of this. I know how to swindle these simple-minded fools and make them feel good about it.

I have many disguises with which to cloak my activities. My favorite is that of a cleric of Tyr. Of course, none of my ruses has ever been uncovered, and it's a good thing. There's a saying: "There are two types of Charlatans—those who are good and those who are dead."

I usually don't stay in one place for very long; it's not safe. By the time the poor fool I've tricked has figured out what happened, I'm long gone.

Once, I agreed to watch over the castle of a good "friend," the rapacious Sir John of Canters, while he went off on a quest. I sold the castle and made off with all the loot before he returned. For now, I am performing sleight-of-hand tricks for mere pocket coins until I meet another "friend." Perhaps tomorrow I will be a powerful mage or a war hero.

I thrive in cities and towns where victims are plentiful and easy to manipulate. Lately, I have been considering the possibility of posing as a thief. Why? So I can accompany a party of adventures in a quest and collect my "share" of the treasure.

Description: Charlatans are masters at manipulating people. Using their high Intelligence and understanding of human nature, Charlatans prey upon the foolish, overconfident, and greedy people around them.

Charlatans often seem bold and boisterous, but they always maintain self-control. The profession of swindling others and making them feel good about it is an age-old practice and none are better at it than Charlatans.

The Charlatan's profession has its downside, too. When a Charlatan's facade is pierced, he is in grave danger, for no one likes to be conned. Then the Charlatan's quick feet may serve him better than his quick wit.

Role: Charlatans are wanderers. They go from town to town, switching from one identity to another, always a step ahead of the last person they swindled. In large cities, Charlatans may be able to live out most of their lives moving from one quarter to the next. When times are tough and no great con comes to mind, Charlatans sometimes perform sleight-of-hand tricks just to get by. Charlatans also have a knack for acquiring jobs that allow them to bluff their way through each day. Charlatans can sometimes be found masquerading as priests, healers, sages, diplomats, powerful mages, and retired heroes.

As player characters, Charlatans are most useful in town-based campaigns or when traveling across inhabited country. Their talents often support the entire party with food, shelter, and minor luxuries. Unfortunately, many of their talents have little use when exploring ruins or wilderness areas. However, they often pose as wizards, warriors, thieves, and sometimes even priests. As NPCs, Charlatans really come into their own.

Secondary Skills: Charlatans can have any secondary skill. However, well over half of all Charlatans are gamblers, jewelers, or limner/painters, for these skills help fill their coin purses in lean times.

Weapon Proficiencies: Charlatans must take dagger, short sword, or long sword as one of their initial weapon proficiencies, as these weapons are used in so many roles that they shouldn't be passed over. At least every second weapon proficiency gained must be one of these three until they are all selected.

A Charlatan selects the rest of his weapons to fill the needs of various roles. For example, if Charlatan decides to masquerade as a powerful warrior, he arms himself with a heavy combat weapon (a two-handed sword, polearm, long bow, or a battle axe) and spends a proficiency slot learning it. This way he can appear to be a skilled and tough fighter. The

Charlatan always uses his proficient weapon in dire situations. If an encounter is less threatening, the Charlatan uses one of the other weapons so as to appear to be a well-rounded fighter (the -3 non-proficiency penalty is easier to hide when attacking monsters with poor Armor Classes).

Nonweapon Proficiencies: *Bonuses:* Acting, Disguise, Forgery, Gaming. *Suggested:* Appraising, Astrology, Healing, Herbalism, Juggling, Reading Lips, Religion, Rope Use, Singing, Ventriloquism.

Armor/Equipment: A Charlatan is allowed to wear any type of armor if a role requires it. Thus, a Charlatan masquerading as a paladin can wear plate mail and carry a shield. But a Charlatan is a finesse character; heavy, bulky armor goes against the grain of his personality. No Charlatan will maintain a role that requires him to wear non-bard armor for more than a few weeks.

Special Benefits:

Charm: Charlatans are aware of their unique charm and flair. They have learned to use this gift to sway the reactions of others. However, such charm must be carefully tailored to a specific audience. Charlatans can affect only a small group of people, no larger in number than their current level.

To be charmed, a group must be in average to high spirits. (You can't charm a merchant who's just been robbed.) The Charlatan must mingle among the intended group and chat for at least 1d10 rounds. After this time, those in the group roll a saving throw vs. paralyzation with a penalty of −1 per three levels of the Charlatan. Those who succeed are unimpressed with the Charlatan and may even find him to be an irritation. If they succeed on a natural 20, they see through the Charlatan's facade.

Those who fail have been caught up in the

Charlatan's tales and find him to be a most remarkable person. The effects of the charm are identical to the wizard spell of the same name. However, it is not magical in any way, and future saving throws are not made based on Intelligence and time. Rather, every time the Charlatan stresses the relationship—by calling for a favor, or requesting delicate information—the paralyzation saving throw is rerolled. The DM can give bonuses or penalties depending on how much stress the request puts on the relationship.

Masquerade: The ability of masquerading requires much study, time, and effort on the part of the Charlatan. This enables a Charlatan to appear to have a specific skill. This is not a disguise, as the proficiency of that name. Rather, it is the ability to appear proficient at the chosen skill. The character picks up the language ('buzz words'), professional mannerisms, and general techniques to help him in his

endeavor.

Unlike the True Bard, the Charlatan only appears to be a jack-of-all trades. He does not study skills to use them, but for the sake of conning others into believing he has them.

The use of this ability is resolved by the DM in much the same manner as an illusion spell. If the performance is not overly suspicious and the characters watching have no reason to disbelieve the bard's ability, then the attempt appears genuine. Otherwise, a saving throw vs. paralyzation is rolled with a −1 penalty per three levels of the Charlatan. Those who succeed realize that the Charlatan is a fraud.

A Charlatan can use his masquerade ability to fake any nonweapon proficiency or secondary skill. Furthermore, if the Charlatan rolls a successful Intelligence check with a −10 penalty, he actually functions as if he really knows the skill or proficiency (for this one check only). Thus, a Charlatan can actually succeed just enough to keep skeptics satisfied.

For example, if Tiel is masquerading as a cleric, she can claim to know the healing proficiency even though she doesn't really have it. Unless those she heals are suspicious, they will believe that the attempts are genuine (if they are suspicious, roll as described two paragraphs prior to this one). First Tiel's player rolls an Intelligence check with a −10 penalty. If that roll succeeds, she next rolls a healing proficiency check. If this check also succeeds, the patient is healed of 1d3 points of damage. If the Intelligence check fails, everyone watching rolls a saving throw vs. paralyzation (with a −1 penalty per three levels of the Charlatan) to notice that the Charlatan is a fraud. If the Intelligence check succeeds but the healing check fails, the patient and onlookers notice only that a valid attempt was made but it just didn't help.

Each time Tiel masquerades as a healer, an Intelligence check is rolled with a -10 penalty. If the check succeeds, a successful healing proficiency check will actually heal 1d3 points of damage.

Detect Fakery: Because Charlatans are so skilled at faking their personalities, lying, and concealing their feelings and reactions, they can see right through false personae and verbal trickery when others attempt them. As the old saying goes, "You can't con a con man." Any time a Charlatan player requests it, he can try to determine if someone is lying, operating under false pretenses (including a masquerade), or swindling him. A Charisma check is rolled. Success means the Charlatan realizes the deception.

Furthermore, a Charisma check with a −10 penalty enables the Charlatan to determine a person's alignment. This requires that the Charlatan speak with and observe the individual for 1d10 rounds.

Swindling: Major cons, such as duping a king into believing that you are a highly respected sage, drawing him into your inner confidence, and then relieving him of the crown jewels, should be done only through role-playing. However, Charlatans hone such skills by constantly performing minor swindles and tricks. These are far too numerous and insignificant to role-play every time. Swindling covers this aspect of a Charlatan's skill repertoire.

By performing various cons, sleight-of-hand, and other deceptions, a Charlatan is often able to walk away from a merchant with far more than a fair deal. The same is true of any common outlay of coins, such as buying meals at a tavern, paying for a room at an inn, and purchasing ordinary items. In instances like these, the Charlatan makes a pick pockets roll. If successful, the cost of the item is multiplied by the percentage rolled; this is what the Charlatan pays. If the roll fails by more than the Charlatan's Charisma, the con is seen through. Swindle rolls above 95 are always detected by the victim.

For example, Tiel tries to swindle a barkeeper for a 10-gp glass of imported wine (Tiel has only six gold coins left). Tiel's pick pockets roll is a 53 and she has a Charisma of 16.

She rolls a 25 and swindles her way into paying only two gold and one electrum for the wine (25% of the original cost). If she had rolled a 54-69 the barkeeper would have noticed the error and politely requested the remainder of the money. On a 70 or above the barkeeper would not only have noticed the error, but he would have realized that Tiel tried to swindle him (with unpleasant consequences for Tiel).

Swindling rolls should not be used for amounts in excess of 10 gp per level of the Charlatan. Such grand swindles require full role-playing.

Special Hindrances: None.

Gallant

Specialty: Romantic Warrior (cavalier).

Qualifications: Standard ability scores. Gallants cannot be neutral evil. Most Gallants are neutral good.

Introduction: *Life as a Gallant? Well, take it from me, Sir Gladiel, that life and love are one and the same. I and my squire, Thorp, have been traveling the Dale Lands since we met some four years ago. Always I am enriched by the charming young ladies I encounter. Between them and the innocent children, I don't see how any man can claim that we live in evil times.*

For the past seven months I've been following the jousting circuit established by his royal highness, Duke Mark of Gunwar Keep. It's been a splendid round of competition. So far I've only won three of my 27 matches, but nearly two dozen of the fairer sex will whisper my name for years to come, for I have entranced them with my honest charm and pure heart.

Unfortunately, there are few men left these days who believe in love for love's sake, who protect the innocent, and who strive for moral purity. Even paladins are too caught up in their own righteousness to live life properly.

It seems that no one realizes that happiness

is the goal of life. Winning and losing is unimportant. All that matters is that you are happy and that your actions do not deprive others of happiness.

Description: There is no character as pure and romantic as the Gallant. He travels the lands on the wings of romance and true love, stealing the hearts of the young and lightening the spirits of the elderly. A Gallant seems to be blessed with a grace and charm not given to others of his race.

Gallants are often mistaken for paladins or cavaliers. They dress and act much like heroic warriors. But they are not driven by blood lust or the desire to slay monsters for the sake of destroying evil. Gallants are romantics at heart. They defend beauty, innocence, and love.

Yet the ways of love and romance cause many a famous Gallant to end his life in tragedy. Shakespeare's Romeo would be such a Gallant.

Role: Gallants travel the lands in search of beauty and true love. Their romantic outlook is such that they can always imagine a purer life just over the next ridge. Thus, they never stay in one place for long. Because of this, most Gallants own a horse to travel the lands.

The pastime of many Gallants is the medieval tournament. Here the skills of jousting, dueling, archery, and other combat practices are honed. Such tournaments draw crowds of young men and women before which the Gallants may perform. Although the warrior classes usually win these tournaments, Gallants often win the hearts of the onlookers and steal the day's glory away from the victorious warriors. Of course, this causes a lot of friction between Gallants and jealous warriors.

When a Gallant goes on an adventure, it is likely the result of some promise to a fair maiden, to retrieve an item of beauty and love, or for some other romantic cause. In

these situations, the Gallant adopts the role of a heroic fighter and charges forward regardless of the dangers that lie ahead.

Secondary Skills: A Gallant should pick his secondary skill from one of the following: Armorer, Bowyer/Fletcher, Groom, Hunter, Leather Worker, Weaponsmith.

Weapon Proficiencies: Gallants must select the jousting lance for use in tournaments. Being the romantic fighters that they are, it is important that Gallants always keep their weapons in perfect order and well polished.

Nonweapon Proficiencies: *Bonuses:* Dancing, Etiquette, Languages (Ancient), Poetry. *Suggested:* Animal Training, Armorer, Artistic Ability, Blacksmithing, Blind-fighting, Bowyer/Fletcher, Languages (Modern), Leatherworking, Musical Instrument, Riding (Land-Based), Reading/Writing, Singing, Weaponsmithing.

Armor/Equipment: Gallants are allowed to wear any form of armor, even those not normally allowed to the core bard. However, Gallants are more interested in quality and appearance than in the armor's actual protection. They will don a gleaming suit of chain mail instead of a dented suit of plate mail. A suit of *studded leather +1* is more appealing to them than the gleaming chain, but *padded leather +4* is even better (*i.e.,* the bigger the magical bonus the better, regardless of the armor type). However, of all forms of armor, elven chain mail is most prized by the Gallant.

The same logic holds true for all of their equipment.

Special Benefits:

Essence of Purity: Because Gallants are so infused with love, beauty, and the aspirations of a romantic, they seem to hang onto life when others would allow it to slip away. Thus, Gallants gain a bonus of 1 hit point each level (in addition to any Constitution bonuses). Furthermore, if a Gallant fails a saving throw that will result in his death, the saving throw is rerolled for a second chance.

Even when a Gallant is slain, he does not immediately drop over dead. Rather, he lingers on long enough to recite one final tragic poem for those who will listen. If the Gallant is slain in combat while defending love, innocence, or beauty (including members of the opposite sex), the Gallant hangs on and fights for another 1d4 rounds or until struck for additional damage equal to his level. Then he recites his poem and dies.

Code of the Gallant: Gallants all live by a code of ethics that has slowly evolved over the years. If a Gallant is true to this code, he gains an inner confidence and peace that results in a +2 bonus that can be applied to either his attack roll, damage roll, Armor Class, or saving throw each round. During the round, the Gallant player may decide to use the +2 bonus at any time before rolling the dice that will be adjusted. Once the bonus is used in a round, it is not available again until next round. The bonus cannot be split into two +1 modifiers.

If a Gallant breaks this code, he loses the +2 bonus until the infraction is remedied. Further, he must seek out a priest who will listen to his transgressions and cast *atonement* upon him (such priests will often require some form of penance).

The Code of the Gallant

The Gallant will . . .

. . . defend lovers, the innocent, and those of the opposite sex and aid them in times of need (unless they are enemies or hostile).

. . . never marry nor solemnly vow to love only one person.

. . . never retreat from combat until allies of the opposite sex have done so first (unless they are fellow Gallants).

. . . never overstay his welcome at any place.

. . . spend at least half of his money on the innocent or romance.

. . . own only what he can carry with him.

Romantic Appeal: The romantic appeal of a Gallant is so strong that non-hostile encounter

reactions are adjusted one level in a more friendly direction unless a successful saving throw vs. paralyzation is rolled with a −1 penalty per three levels of the Gallant. However, if the encounter includes mixed genders, those of the same sex as the Gallant will actually be adjusted one level in the opposite direction if they succeed on their saving throw (as jealousy rears its ugly head).

Poetic Charm: A Gallant who directs his attention to one person of the opposite sex can attempt to win that person's heart. This requires the Gallant to perform many subtle acts of wit and charm. Among these acts must be the recital of at least one poem concerning the person. The entire effort takes a minimum of 1d10 turns, after which the person rolls a saving throw vs. paralyzation with a −1 penalty per three levels of the Gallant. Failure means that the person is affected as if the Gallant cast a *charm* spell on him or her.

The effect is not magical and doesn't wear off over time, unless the Gallant exploits or treats the person badly. Each such abuse results in another saving throw being rolled to break the Gallant's charm. The Dungeon Master may apply adjustments based on the situation. For example, if a Gallant asks a princess to tell him where the king's treasure is hidden, she will gain a saving throw adjusted by the degree of loyalty she has to her father. Striking the princess (something greatly out of character for a Gallant) to gain this information is likely to result in at least a +5 bonus to break free of the Gallant's charm.

Special Hindrances: A Gallant is a wanderer who never builds a stronghold. Nor does he attract followers at 9th level. At 5th level, however, a Gallant gains a squire (a 1st-level fighter). This squire is absolutely devoted to the Gallant, maintains his equipment in top order, and accompanies him on all of his quests. If a Gallant's squire is slain, a new squire arrives as soon as the Gallant acquires two more experience levels.

Gypsy-bard

Specialty: Dance/Instruments/Singing.
Qualifications: Standard ability scores. Gypsy-bards cannot be lawful neutral. Elves can become Gypsy-bards able to advance to the 9th level.
Introduction: *I'm known as Madraime, and I'm a Gypsy lady. Oh, I'm not what most people would call a typical Gypsy. Within the society of gypsies, there are many different types of individuals. I am what is known as a Gypsy-bard, performing-Gypsy, or dancing-girl.*

I travel with my father's caravan, performing for the locals of a region as we pass through. When I'm not singing and dancing for the outsiders, I often entertain those of my caravan in the evening hours. There is nothing as lovely as spending an evening among my own kind, dancing, singing, and enjoying the company of those who understand the world.

Like all Gypsies, I realize that humans, elves, dwarves, and others were meant to lead lives of inner discovery, peaceful joy, and association with nature. I know that many people distrust Gypsies, calling us thieves and worse. This occurs because we Gypsies are misunderstood. Our beliefs are so pure and so natural that they are hard for outsiders to understand.

For example, as a Gypsy, I understand that ownership of an item exists only so long as the item is not ignored or forgotten. If I lay down my magical dagger, walk away, and one of my brothers should find it, the dagger is then his. If I want it back I must trade him something in exchange.

How can anyone claim to own something that they aren't using or aren't holding? What gives a king the right to say that he owns the land of a country? The land was there before he or his family ever lived, and it will be there long after they are all dead. Likewise, how can a farmer claim that he owns the sheep that feed upon the land? These sheep exist because

they eat the fruit of the land, and the land belongs to no one. The ways of outsiders are very odd indeed.

We Gypsies are a peaceful folk who wish only to travel upon the good earth, laugh, sing, and live the ways of life.

Description: This kit defines the role of the bard in Gypsy life. Gypsies can be treated as a coherent society or as any group with a nomadic lifestyle.

Gypsies are often called "forest nomads." They travel the lands in caravans comprising carts, wagons, horses, and the Gypsy folk. These people are well known for their strange Gypsy music and dances. Some caravans survive by entertaining the communities they encounter. Not all gypsies are bards; the Gypsy-bard is only one type of character that fills the ranks of a Gypsy band.

Gypsy ways are strange to others and poorly understood by most. They do not recognize the existence of private property. The fruits of the land belong to all. If there is not enough to go around, it is easy enough to pack the wagons and move along. Likewise, Gypsies use only what they need and do not seek wealth or possessions for their own sake, or for the influence or power that they bring. They do not have a king or queen, although sometimes they will lay claim to these titles to gain advantage in bartering (when outsiders believe this, the Gypsies take it as proof of their gullibility and stupidity).

Gypsy-bards have an entire collection of unconventional concepts that make up their philosophy of life:

• Gypsy-bards are free thinkers. For example, many do not marry, seeking companionship only for as long as both parties agree to the arrangement.

• Gypsy-bards love nature.

• Many Gypsy-bards don't worship deities (although certain deities may look over them). Instead, they worship the concepts of nature, free will, and life.

• Gypsy-bards draw their energies from their free will, their brethren, and from their natural surroundings.

• A Gypsy-bard is loyal to and protects his friends, but friendship must be earned, and it is not gained easily.

• Possession and ownership are the same.

• Money is useless unless it brings you pleasure; trade is a better form of commerce.

• You should always dress and act naturally and comfortably.

• The rigid customs and beliefs of non-Gypsies are foolish and should be ignored.

Only a fellow Gypsy truly understands the Gypsy way of life. Others wrongly classify Gypsies as thieves, beggars, carnival people, nomads, or any number of other erroneous names. If a label must be used, the most accurate is "free-men."

Role: Gypsy-bards wander the land, experiencing life as they go. They travel until they find something of interest: a beautiful glade, an interesting village, an audience to sing and dance before, or someone who wants to trade with them. Then they establish a temporary camp and remain until their need to see more of the world overpowers their desire to stay.

An adventuring Gypsy-bard may be on a personal quest to locate some special animal or flower for the "Gypsy queen," or he could simply be out to experience the great wonders that appear along the adventuring path. In any event, a Gypsy-bard always has a purpose and philosophy to his adventuring, even if it is "to wander for the sake of wandering."

Secondary Skills: Forester, Gambler, Groom, Hunter, Jeweler, Teamster/Freighter, Trader/Barterer.

Weapon Proficiencies: Gypsy-bards must take either dagger or knife, and their first sword (if any is ever taken) must be either the khopesh or scimitar. Gypsy-bards cannot become proficient in the following weapons: battle axe, lance (any), polearm (any), trident, two-handed sword, bastard sword, or warhammer. All other weapons are available

to them.

Nonweapon Proficiencies: *Bonuses:* Dancing, Direction Sense, Languages (modern—Gypsy), Musical Instrument (tambourine, violin, mandolin). *Suggested:* Ancient History, Astrology, Cooking, Craft Instrument, Disguise, Fire-Building, Gaming, Herbalism, Hunting, Juggling, Singing, Spellcraft, Survival, Tracking, Ventriloquism, Weather Sense.

Armor/Equipment: Gypsy-bards can wear only leather, padded, studded leather, hide, or elven chain mail. The other types are too noisy, bulky, and are considered to be impure and unnatural.

Both male and female Gypsy-bards love to wear gaudy jewelry. Their garments are typically loose-fitting and comfortable.

Special Benefits:

Animal Rapport: Gypsy-bards are nearly druidical in their ability to associate with animals. They automatically gain the proficiencies of animal handling, animal lore, animal training, and riding (land-based). Furthermore, their training and riding skills extend to any animal with which they become familiar.

At 5th, 10th and 15th levels, Gypsy-bards gain the ability to cause certain spell-like effects, each once per day. At 5th level, they are able to cause the effects of *animal friendship* by speaking kindly in the secret language of their own (Gypsy dialect). At 10th level, they can concentrate and gain the benefits of a *locate animals or plants* spell. Finally, at 15th level, they gain the *speak with animals* ability.

Allure of the Gypsies: Certain Gypsy songs and dances are very alluring and can have powerful influences over those who willingly listen or take part. For such performances to function, a group of at least three Gypsy-bards must be performing together, or the audience must be willingly participating.

These performances take at least 1d10 turns. The effect of such performances can be identical to any one spell of the enchantment/charm school (as determined by the dance). However, at least one of the main performers must be high enough level to cast the spell. It is not required that the performer have the spell memorized, but he must have personal knowledge of it (in his spell books; roll a successful "chance to learn spell" check). The spell range, duration, and other effects that vary by caster level are determined by the eligible performer's level, as if he actually cast the desired spell.

Fortune Telling: By using any magical item suited for scrying or divining the future, such as a *crystal ball* or *medallion of ESP*, a Gypsy-bard can gain the benefits of an *augury* spell. Each day, the Gypsy-bard can ask one question per five levels of experience (rounded up). Note that Gypsy-bards can even tell fortunes by using magical scrying items that are not otherwise usable by them. For example, *crystal balls* are usable only by wizards, and not even a Gypsy-bard can gain the typical benefits of the ball. However, by looking into one and concentrating, a Gypsy-bard can ask one *augury*-style yes/no question per five levels, during that day.

Besides items suited for scrying and divining the future, Gypsy-bards are able to perform the same feat with a *deck of many things*. Additionally, when a *deck of many things* is used by the Gypsy-bard for this purpose, the cards turned never affect him for good or bad. Drawing the void or the donjon card will not cause the deck to vanish. However, the deck still functions normally when used for purposes other than the augury.

Psionics: An unusually large number of Gypsy-bards are psionic. If the optional psionics rules are used (see *The Complete Psionics Handbook*), all player character Gypsy-bards should be wild talent psionics. Psionic talents are determined by whatever method the DM prefers.

Special Hindrances: A Gypsy-bard's climb walls ability works best when climbing trees. They are not skilled at climbing cliffs, building walls, or cave walls; they suffer a 25% penalty when scaling these surfaces.

Herald

Specialty: Linguist/Orator.
Qualifications: Standard ability scores. Demihumans can become Heralds of up to 6th level.

Introduction: *Hello, my name is Bard, James Bard, and I'm a Herald working for His Majesty, the king.*

My duties are of the utmost importance to the king and to the continued vitality of the kingdom, for I am secretly in charge of the King's private men-at-arms and personal bodyguards. If the king's life is in danger, I am responsible for ensuring his safety.

My public image is one of party-goer, ladies' man, and general royal busybody. I frequent all the best parties in town. The king often ensures that I am invited. At these functions, I meet important people and use my fantastic communication skills and intellect to uncover potential plots against the throne.

When I'm not partying, the public finds me at the castle gate. When a party comes to the castle, I use my knowledge to identify their Herald or banner and call out their name, such as: "Duke Amenga and entourage from Castle Peledge." This is a useful service, but my real purpose is to identify these visitors, assess their potential threat to the king, and act accordingly.

Enough talk, I must be off to chat with that strange-looking man entering the gates over there.

Description: Heralds make their living by uncovering hidden truths. If a royal family has a closely guarded secret, a Herald will undoubtedly discover it. In the struggle for land and power among kingdoms, the Herald is a key force. A good Herald knows who is plot-

ting against his king and why.

Heralds are confident and well-versed in matters of social etiquette. They often gather their information at royal events, such as balls and other celebrations. They are often mistaken for nobility; thus, they can easily make their way past guards. Heralds dress in the latest and most expensive fashions of the day. They prefer silk and bright colors. Members of the opposite sex are often attracted to Heralds by their self-confident manner and slight arrogance.

One thing is certain, Heralds are some of the most competent communicators around. They can speak dozens of languages, understand sophisticated words, locate a person's home village by his dialect, and can read almost everything they get their hands on.

Role: There are two types of Heralds. One travels from place to place, relating current events across the land. They sell their tales of travel and the news they learn to those who will listen. Most medieval commoners cannot read or write, so it is up to such Heralds to relate local events.

The other type of Herald secretly serves a king. It is the royal Herald's duty to uncover plots against the king and royal family. The royal Herald is quick witted and fast talking. Heralds of this stature often have a reputation that precedes them. They are recognized and feared by their foes. Thus, they must occasionally deal with assassination attempts at inconvenient times (for instance, a *delayed blast fireball* under the bed). Royal courts often employ them to preside over jousting tournaments, announce the arrival of important foreign envoys, and for personal counsel.

Heralds turn to the adventuring life for several reasons. Primary among them are the fantastic stories that can be related from such ventures. "News" has a very broad meaning in the campaign world, and tales of a daring band of heroes braving unknown horrors not only qualifies, but often draws a larger crowd than local gossip.

The royal Herald might be sent by his king on an undercover fact-finding mission—for instance, to investigate a rumor that Zhentil Keep is secretly funding an orc uprising in the south. Often, a Herald's communication skills will prove invaluable on such quests.

Secondary Skills: Groom, Hunter, Jeweler, Limner/Painter, Scribe.

Weapon Proficiencies: Heralds are not restricted in this area.

Nonweapon Proficiencies: *Bonuses:* Etiquette, Heraldry, Local History, Reading/Writing. *Suggested:* Languages (ancient or modern), Musical Instrument (horn family). At least half of a Herald's nonweapon proficiencies must be spent in learning languages.

Armor/Equipment: Standard.

Special Benefits:

Identify Rumors: Heralds are always aware of their surroundings and have picked up the skills necessary to stay atop local events. Any

time rumors are generated for player characters, Heralds learn twice as many as a normal character. Heralds are also able to determine the validity of a rumor. A Charisma check is rolled; if it succeeds, the Herald knows whether the rumor is true or false. Even if a rumor table isn't included in a given adventure, the Dungeon Master should make up at least one rumor per three levels of the Herald and inform him of the rumors at the adventure's onset.

Local Lore: After snooping about an inhabited area, a Herald is able to learn who the important people are, what most of the buildings are used for, the quality of certain establishments, *etc.* It takes a Herald one day per 1,000 inhabitants to gain a good information base. Of course, a Herald could concentrate on a specific quarter of town or neighborhood and accomplish the task much faster.

Once a Herald is done scouting, he can recall the name of an important official if he rolls a successful Intelligence check. If the check is successful with a −2 penalty, he can identify the person on sight. This roll can also be used if the Herald player wants to know other local lore, such as where to go for the best food in town, what neighborhoods are dangerous at night, what time the city watch rotates, or which local sage is said to be most reliable. If the check is a 20, the Herald believes he knows the desired information, but the Dungeon Master actually makes up some false tale for the player.

This ability must be carefully judged by the Dungeon Master. Penalties should be applied based upon the information's local significance. It is unlikely that a Herald will know the name of a typical citizen in a large city (a −10 penalty might be appropriate). However, the name of the king's horse is likely a well-known fact (no penalty).

Basal Communication: As stated above, Heralds are master linguists. In fact, they can often communicate with races that are of low Intelligence or better and have a spoken language, even if the Herald does not speak that language. The Herald incorporates bits and pieces of fundamental root languages, certain universal gestures, and common expressions to get his meaning across. For the Herald to perform such difficult communication, the "listener" must be within ten feet, clearly visible, and there must be no distractions (including combat).

Success is determined by succeeding with a read languages roll (even though the communication is rarely in written form). A separate roll is needed to send or receive ideas. Thus, it is possible for a Herald to understand a being, but be unable to communicate his own ideas (or vice versa).

Persuade Crowd: A Herald can affect the mood of a crowd by telling them true (or slightly altered) local rumors and news. The Herald must be able to speak the crowd's language to use this ability. To determine a crowd's mood or opinion on a given topic, use Table 59 in the *DMG*.

After 1d10 minutes, those listening to the Herald's words are allowed a saving throw vs. paralyzation, with a −1 penalty per three levels of the Herald. Those who fail have their reactions adjusted one level in favor of the Herald's opinion. Those who succeed have their reactions adjusted one level in the opposite direction.

A Herald could attempt to persuade a crowd not to eat at the Skinned Dog Tavern until dragon eggs are back on the menu, to cast stones at the cruel teamster Tornack, or to go and plunder the local granaries. Of course, reactions can be altered only one level by this method. For example, if everyone is indifferent to the fact that Tornack whips his horses cruelly, the Herald will at most persuade them to be cautious about using the teamster's wagons to haul their goods.

Special Hindrances: None.

Jester

Specialty: Pantomime/Acting/Dancing/ Jokes.

Qualifications: Standard ability scores, except that Dexterity must be at least 14. Jesters must be of any chaotic alignment, since no mind attuned to law and order could possibly sustain such an odd personality. Gnomes may advance to 15th level as Jesters, while halflings cannot rise above 8th level.

Introduction: *My name is Marigold the Mirthful, and I am proud to be called a Jester, for I am one of the greatest fools in all the kingdom. Being a fool is not all bad, for who else can poke fun at the most powerful people around without meeting the gallows or worse?*

Indeed, I lead the perfect life. The king puts me up in a fantastic little room at the top of the East Tower. When the morning sun comes through my little window, I rise and don my charming gear. Then I spring and dance down the 40-foot-long spiral staircase to the main hall. All the while, my costume bells are jingling and I can hear the moans and groans as the court wakes from my passing. Next, I tumble down all the castle's halls and awaken the rest of the royal patrons.

Unless there are foreign envoys to be entertained at noon, I am off until evening. I wander about, keeping the young folk happy and feeding the chickens and the castle's two war dogs. Then I usually find a comfortable willow tree and lie down for a short nap.

Most evenings, the king invites me in to entertain him, his family, and his guests. I dance about, act foolish, juggle a bit, perform some minor acrobatics, pretend to get burnt by the fireplace, and tell jokes that I made up while lying under the willow tree.

So you see, I live in the king's castle and actually do little or no work. What a lucky life! Of course, the real fun occurs when foreigners arrive. I always make sure they leave the king's court with fewer goods than they came *in with. I would hate to see them lug all that gold, silver, and jewelry clear back to their homelands.*

Description: Jesters are known by many names: fools, clowns, jokers, buffoons, *etc.* The Jester kit covers them all. Jesters are comedians at heart. They love to have a good time and enjoy sharing their mirth and merriment with others (even when they aren't welcomed). Most people enjoy having a Jester about, as they raise morale, entertain, and make great scapegoats when problems arise.

Jesters are flamboyant, outrageous, and ridiculous. Many sages believe that Jesters live in a constant state of borderline insanity. It is known that they live for attention and feel relaxed only when they are the focus of events.

Role: Jesters are often hired by noblemen for entertainment. They dance, prance, and jump about while the more civilized look on and laugh at the fools. More often than not, these noblemen are paying the price for their entertainment, as the Jester is liable to make off with a piece of gold for every laugh he hears. Other Jesters serve as clowns in traveling carnivals or circuses. And of course every community has its local fool.

Jesters rarely take up the adventuring life. (PC Jesters are the obvious exceptions.) Their motivations for doing so will have to be carefully constructed to maintain realism. A Jester may be sentenced to escort a group of heroes on a dangerous quest as punishment for a joke about the king's nose (throwing him in jail would hardly be appropriate). A Jester might be assigned to accompany a band on a grim and deadly adventure, to combat the gloom and dread that will be encountered. Whatever the reason, having a Jester in the party will certainly result in more than one good laugh.

Secondary Skills: Any.

Weapon Proficiencies: Jesters spend most of their lives entertaining others by playing the role of a fool or clown. Large weapons do not fit into this role. Thus Jesters may become proficient only in the blowgun, hand cross-

bow, dagger, dart, hand axe, javelin, knife, quarterstaff, scourge, sling, short sword, and whip.

Nonweapon Proficiencies: *Bonuses:* Acting, Dancing, Juggling, Tumbling. *Suggested:* Crowd Working, Disguise, Jumping, Musical Instrument, Poetry, Singing, Ventriloquism.

Armor/Equipment: Jesters may wear only the following types of armor: leather, padded, studded leather, or elven chain mail. Other types of armor do not fit the image of fools.

Jesters almost always act and dress in the most outlandish manner. Even when danger is imminent, Jesters still hop around in their flashy suits with tassels and foppish hats.

Special Benefits:

Fool's Luck: It is amazing to most that Jesters can survive in any situation. They are careless, foolish, and given to whimsical decisions. It is fool's luck that has saved many a Jester's life.

Jesters receive a +1 bonus (+5% on percentile rolls) to most die rolls. This includes saving throws, initiative, surprise, proficiency checks, thief skill checks, ability checks, and ability sub-checks (*e.g.*, bend bars/lift gates, resurrection survival, and so on). The fool's luck also adds a +1 bonus to the Jester's Armor Class.

About the only die rolls that the fool's luck ability doesn't affect are attack rolls, damage rolls, initial character generation rolls, and Hit Die rolls.

Jesting: Jesting is the art of projecting meaning and mood through the use of body motions. By jesting (or gesturing), a Jester may communicate a single sentence each round to anyone who rolls a successful Wisdom check with a −5 penalty. Such communication is totally silent and does not rely upon a shared language. The Jester must use his entire body for the communication; thus, he must be fully visible and within 30 feet for communication to take place.

Jesting may be done to taunt or tease. Such jesting affects only those who are within 30

feet of the Jester and who are able to fully view him. This form of jesting causes those being jested at to roll a saving throw vs. paralyzation, with a −1 penalty per three levels of the Jester. Those who fail must immediately try to physically strike the Jester for as long as the jesting continues. The effect ends when the jesting ends. Combat strategy is ignored by those who are affected. They recklessly pass by more dangerous targets in an attempt to attack the Jester. Jesting is thus a wonderful way to break the ranks of enemy forces.

Joking: The practice of creating and telling jokes has been elevated to an art form by the Jester; this skill can be used for many special purposes. Jokes are told in an attempt to alter encounter reactions. For any form of joke to function, the Jester must speak a language known by the recipient of the joke. Furthermore, the Jester must be within easy verbal range of the recipient.

Such jokes require 1d10 rounds to tell, after which the audience must roll a saving throw vs. paralyzation with a −1 penalty per three levels of the Jester. Those who fail have their reactions adjusted one level in the direction desired by the Jester. However, those who succeed take the joke the wrong way and have their reactions adjusted one level in the opposite direction.

Finally, a joke told at just the right moment can dispel the effects of fear. Such a joke requires a round to tell and enables all those affected by fear (normal or magical) to roll a second saving throw to avoid the fear (note that those affected by the fear do not immediately run away, but remain until the joke is told). If no first saving throw was allowed, then the saving throw is rolled vs. spell.

A Jester's Mind: Jesters are immune to attacks that cause insanity. Jesters also gain a saving throw bonus equal to their level vs. wizard spells of the enchantment/charm school and priest spells of the charm sphere. (A saving throw of 1 always fails, however.)

Furthermore, any attempt to read a Jester's mind has a percentage chance equal to the Jester's level of causing *confusion* in the mind reader (treat as if under the effect of a *confusion* spell).

Special Hindrances: None.

Notes: Jesters can be a lot of fun if properly played with the right gaming group. However, this character kit can be devastating to an overly serious campaign. It is strongly suggested that both DMs and players discuss the ramifications of the kit and how it will fit into the game if allowed.

Jongleur

Specialty: Juggler/Acrobat.

Qualifications: Jongleurs must have a Dexterity of 14 or more (other ability scores, standard). Gnomes can advance to the 9th level as Jongleurs. Halflings can attain 12th level.

Introduction: *Yes, I am a Jongleur. My stage name is Jonclaur the Jongleur, and that will do for now. I travel across the Flanaess with a small carnival band. I believe you have already met one of my companions, Dark. He's good with knives and swords, but his personality matches his name a little too much for me.*

When our troupe puts on a show, I tend to draw the largest and most consistent audience. In particular, families and village thieves enjoy watching my act. Families watch because my juggling, pole vaulting, acrobatics, and tightrope walking amazes them (and occasionally fills them with concern when my act looks particularly hazardous). The thieves come to study my actions. Many thieves can pole vault, walk tightropes, and perform various feats of acrobatics, but none have my skill. In a way, it's a form of research for them.

And it is true, though I hate to admit it, that my talents are occasionally put to less-than-honorable uses. On one of the last few days of our show, a large part of our troupe often stages some complex burglary. My skills are often invaluable. I can vault across moats or into upper story windows that are protected by walls coated with contact poison. If a mansion is guarded by dogs, I use a crossbow to fire a line from a nearby building, then walk across it. Of course, I rarely keep my share of this booty. Instead, I usually donate it to the local orphanage or poorhouse.

Well, nice chatting with you, but I must get back. My second act is about to begin.

Description: Jongleurs are loosely based upon the French entertainers of the same name. They are masters at manipulating small items with their hands. They can catch and juggle almost anything. On top of this they are skilled acrobats, able to traverse tightropes, turn flips, polevault, and perform any number of acrobatic feats. Their agility provides them with great defensive resources.

Role: As entertainers, most Jongleurs are typically found accompanying carnivals or

circuses. A troupe of Jongleurs can put on a remarkable show all by themselves. They often perform in taverns or clubs, using their arts to draw in the crowd and captivate them long enough for the barkeeper (as well as the Jongleurs) to drain the crowd's purses. Of course, a few free-lancers work the streets out of greed or need.

Jongleurs are useful adventuring allies; their skills are invaluable when the going gets tough. They are able to squeeze into places where nobody else can go without the aid of magic. Finally, their skill at avoiding certain traps makes them excellent scouts.

Secondary Skills: Any.

Weapon Proficiencies: Jongleurs can use all hurled weapons. A hurled weapon is any weapon that can be thrown (this does not include bows, blowguns, or other missile weapons that are fired or shot). Otherwise, Jongleurs are restricted to the following weapons: polearms, quarterstaff, sling, staff sling, and whip. All of these weapons can be used in their performances. For example, they can juggle daggers, pole vault with polearms, and balance with spears or quarterstaves.

Nonweapon Proficiencies: *Bonuses:* Juggling, Jumping, Tightrope Walking, Tumbling. *Suggested:* Direction Sense, Endurance, Poetry, Rope Use, Running.

Armor/Equipment: If a Jongleur wears any type of armor other than leather, studded leather, padded, or elven chain mail, he cannot use any of the following special benefits. All other forms of armor are simply too restrictive or bulky for the Jongleur to properly perform.

Jongleurs tend to dress in rather flashy colors. However, they don't take this to the extremes that Jesters do. They avoid large capes, robes, and other garments that can catch or tangle during movement. Of course, this does not mean that a Jongleur is going to wear a flaming red suit that sparkles in the dimmest of lights when exploring ancient ruins. They prefer flash and fanfare, but they aren't stupid.

Special Benefits:

Extended Proficiencies: Because Jongleurs are extremely skilled at all forms of juggling and acrobatics, they gain certain special benefits to their bonus proficiencies.

Juggling:

• The Jongleur adds his level to the attack roll when trying to catch small items.

• Missile or hurled weapons too large to catch can be deflected by using the juggling proficiency.

Jumping:

• The Jongleur doubles his level for all jumping calculations.

• The character can use poles up to 20 feet longer than himself.

• Vaults can be made with a 15-foot run. The pole need not be dropped if a second proficiency check is successful.

Tightrope Walking:
- All penalties are halved, dropping fractions (*i.e.*, −5 for one-inch surfaces, −2 for two- to six-inch surfaces, and −2 attack roll penalty).
- Use of a balancing rod provides a +4 bonus.

Tumbling:
- The +4 Armor Class bonus applies during any round in which initiative is won, even if the Jongleur opts to attack later that round.
- No proficiency check is required to reduce falling damage. However, a successful proficiency check doubles the falling distances (*i.e.*, no damage up to 20 feet and only half damage up to 120 feet).

Dodge: Jongleurs are amazingly agile and have very quick reflexes. This enables them to jump free of many potentially harmful situations if a successful saving throw vs. paralyzation is rolled. The only bonus allowed to the save is the defensive bonus for high Dexterity.

If the attempted dodge fails, the Jongleur suffers the full effects of the danger. No other saving throw can be rolled to avoid the threat, as the dodge takes the place of all other saving throws. The benefit of dodging is that all harm is completely avoided, whereas many successful saving throws result in half damage. Of course, the Jongleur player can opt to skip the dodge attempt in favor of any normally allowed saving throws.

Dodging does not affect missile weapons or hurled weapons, personal spells (those that affect only one person) directed specifically at the Jongleur, or spells that have no physical effect to dodge (such as *hold person*).

Situations that can be avoided include falls (into pits, through illusionary floors, down sliding stairways traps, *etc.*), being struck from above (by ceiling blocks, rocks, piercers, collapses, *etc.*), area-effect spells that can be dodged (*lightning bolt, web, fireball, etc.*), and any other situation that the Dungeon Master feels could be avoided by a sudden agile leap (possibly breath weapons). Of course, if a jump to safety is impossible, the Jongleur cannot attempt a dodge. Note that Jongleurs are also able to climb walls and might avoid certain situations by clinging to a wall.

Entertain Crowd: By juggling, performing flips, or displaying his acrobatic talents, a Jongleur can influence the reactions of an audience. This ability is similar to the True Bard's influence reactions ability.

As with that ability, the crowd cannot be attacking or about to attack. The Jongleur must perform for 1d10 rounds, after which all non-player characters viewing the performance must roll saving throws vs. paralyzation (split large audiences into groups of 10 and roll one saving throw for each group). The saving throw is rolled with a −1 penalty per three levels of the bard (round down). Those failing have their reactions adjusted one level in a more friendly direction, as per Table 59 in the *DMG*.

Unlike True Bards, Jongleurs cannot attempt to worsen the reactions of a crowd (it is very difficult to juggle or walk a tightrope in an offensive manner). However, if the crowd saves with a natural 1, the onlookers disapprove of the Jongleur and their reactions actually worsen by one level.

Special Hindrances: Jongleurs do not gain the 10th-level ability to use any written magical item.

Loremaster

Specialty: Chronicler/Historian.
Qualifications: Loremasters must have an Intelligence and Wisdom of 14 or more (other ability scores are standard). Elves can advance up to 12th level as Loremasters.
Introduction: *You want to know about history, lost civilizations, and other fascinating topics? Well, let me introduce myself, I'm Ashlan, a gray elf and self-proclaimed Loremaster.*

I guess I've been poring over old tomes, exploring ancient ruins, and searching for lost civilizations for the past 150 years or so. And I've learned many important things. Did you know that, in ages past, the entire inland plains were covered with a vast forest of piñon and pine trees? Humans were scarce back then and elves ruled the land. Oh, that must have been a beautiful time! Then there came the great goblin wars, when all goblinkind rose up in anger after being pushed far below ground. They were lead by Trogundak, perhaps the largest and most evil troll shaman who ever lived.

But I forget myself. You want to know about me and not the past. Well, I'm called a recluse by most of the villagers around here. This is actually far from the truth. I love people, all people. I love to study about their past history in an attempt to understand them better than they understand themselves. Then I try to teach them about their past and educate them so they won't commit the mistakes of their forefathers all over again.

I guess I do seem a bit odd to the average soul, seeing as how I'm always poking around cemeteries, old churches, ruins, and private libraries. Most people can't figure me out. Some think I'm a cleric, others believe me to be a simple hermit, and there are those who call me sage or wizard. It is true that I can speak over half a dozen languages, but I'm just a Loremaster, that's all.

Remember, study your past; it can be the most powerful tool you have.

Description: Loremasters are romantically entranced by the past. They believe in the circular nature of history and relate the lessons of ancient times to the problems of the present to help guide their people along the path to the future. As Loremasters proceed through life, they record the events of their own times for posterity.

Loremasters love to relate the lessons of history to those who will listen. However, they are often viewed as being more reclusive and eccentric than wizards. Their preoccupation with old tomes, arcane lore, ancient languages, and lost civilizations dominates their lives, when they aren't putting on an oratorical performance. From their research, Loremasters gain unique wisdom and insight, allowing them to identify certain magical items, understand ancient writings and languages, gain special benefits in the arcane lore of magic, and incite crowds to action.

Role: There is a fine line between Loremaster and sage. So fine that many Loremasters call themselves sages and are rarely questioned about it. However, true sages are knowledge specialists who concentrate their efforts into mastering a specific field such as mushrooms, elven swords, and so on. Loremasters are fond of any aspect of history that makes a good story.

Many Loremasters are travelers who wander the lands searching for great historical tales and facts to relate to crowds. In order to gain the substance of their tales, Loremasters often take up adventuring. Unlike many other adventurers, Loremasters are not simply seeking gold or magic. Rather, they are searching for a new legend or tale. Loremasters are the first to open old tomes, read the runes on passage walls, and record the general events of an adventure.

Secondary Skills: Limner/Painter, Navigator, Scribe (better than a third of all Loremasters are scribes.)

Weapon Proficiencies: Due to their great interest in knowledge and their concentration on the past, Loremasters bother to learn only the lightest and simplest of weapons. They are limited to selecting weapon proficiencies for blowgun, dagger, dart, hand crossbow, knife, quarterstaff, sling, and staff sling.

Nonweapon Proficiencies: *Bonuses:* Ancient History, Languages (ancient), Navigation, Reading/Writing. *Suggested:* Animal Lore, Artistic Ability, Astrology, Direction Sense, Engineering, Etiquette, Heraldry, Languages (modern), Local History, Musical In-

strument, Religion, Spellcraft, Weather Sense.

Armor/Equipment: Loremasters spend their time studying arcane tomes and ancient civilizations. They do not bother to practice the use of heavy armor. Thus Loremasters can use only leather armor.

Loremasters generally dress and act much like wizards.

Special Benefits:

Legend Lore: Loremasters gain the same legend lore ability as True Bards. This ability works in similar fashion, with the following exception: All of the optional rules suggested for the True Bard's legend lore ability are required for the Loremaster.

Arcane Lore: Through their devoted study of the past, Loremasters come across numerous texts on the arcane lore of magic. They read all of these, hoping that some great tale will be uncovered. Loremasters eventually gain a fundamental understanding of many strange magical items not normally usable by the bard class. Thus, Loremasters can attempt to use any magical item. A Wisdom check is rolled; if it is successful, the Loremaster successfully uses the magical item in question. This does not mean that the Loremaster fully understands the operation of the item, only that his attempt to use it in this particular way is successful.

Loremasters also pore over scrolls and spell books whenever they get the chance. This enhances their understanding of magical spells so much that they memorize and cast spells as if they were one level higher. Thus, a 1st-level Loremaster casts spells the same way as a 2nd-level True Bard.

Persuasion: Usually Loremasters recite their collections of historical fables and legends to a crowd simply to entertain and educate. Although these oral performances are wonderful to hear, they do not necessarily

have any direct impact upon the crowd.

When a Loremaster wishes to affect the mood or actions of an audience, he uses his great skills of verbal persuasion, oratory, and rhetoric. He might relate the legend of the horrible massacre of Tothar Keep by lizard men in an attempt to incite the crowd to hate and despise lizard men.

Using such persuasion takes at least 1d10 rounds. All who are listening to and can understand the Loremaster must roll a saving throw vs. paralyzation with a −1 penalty for every three levels of the Loremaster. Those who fail have their reactions adjusted one level up or down (as desired by the Loremaster). Those who succeed are not inspired by the tale, and those few who roll a natural 20 strongly disagree with the tale and have their reactions adjusted one level in the opposite direction.

Etymology: Loremasters can make their read languages attempt twice if the language in question is an ancient one (a language no longer spoken). They can also use their read languages ability to decipher runes, glyphs, pictograms, ideograms, or any other form of ancient visual communication.

Even though a Loremaster cannot be proficient in a newly encountered ancient language, if he makes his Ancient Languages proficiency check, he understands the basics of the ancient language. Elementary use of the language is gained, allowing for written or even spoken communication at one-tenth the normal rate.

Special Hindrances: None.

Meistersinger

Specialty: Pied Piper/Animal Charmer.
Qualifications: Standard ability scores. Elves can become Meistersingers and reach 15th level.
Introduction: *Welcome to Great Wood. My name is Shellana and I will be guiding you through this beautiful forest. I've lived here for as long as I can remember. My father is a ranger who patrols the forest and my mother maintains a small cottage for us all.*

My dearest friends are Simbiom, a red barn owl, and Moshma, a jet black panther. They accompany me wherever I go. And where is that? Well, I don't really have a job as most people would define it. I often help the rangers who patrol the Great Wood. They are concerned with the security of some kingdom or other and want to keep the forest free of spies and evil monsters. I help them by reporting any strange people or creatures I encounter.

But my real goal is to keep the forest and its animals safe from the encroachment of "civilization." Greedy furriers and loggers and wasteful travelers are my enemies. I have freed countless animals from live traps, have broken numerous logging saws, and have scared off several dozen city folk this year.

I secretly work with the druids. Together we have kept the forest and its creatures relatively safe from harm. But our jobs grow more and more difficult as new villages keep popping up near the forest's edge. And with that said, I must go and plant some more trees before Simbiom eats all of my nuts.

Description: Meistersingers wander the woodlands, mountains, and deserts, seeking out those who will listen to their songs. Unlike other bards, Meistersingers rarely perform for humankind. They tailor their music to the tunes of nature. Their audiences are the birds, the bees, and the behemoths.

Meistersingers have wandered unsettled lands since the dawn of mankind. Loremasters tell tales about how the ancient dryads and nymphs would find lost human children and teach them the ways of the forest. Others were taken in by druids. Over the years, these children of nature have evolved into a definable class of character—the Meistersinger. Whether these tales are true or not, Meistersingers do exist.

The concerns of Meistersingers center around nature, especially animals. Lawful

neutral, true neutral, and chaotic neutral Meistersingers see themselves as one with nature (although each views the structure of nature differently). They protect animals as humans protect those of their society. Neutral good Meistersingers look upon animals as innocent children who should be isolated and protected from the harsh and uncaring realms of civilization. Neutral evil Meistersingers see animals as subjects to be controlled and exploited. They use animals as some lords use slaves. True neutral Meistersingers are closest to druids in the way they look upon animals.

Role: Meistersingers are the mortal enemies of ruthless and profiteering hunters, trappers, and fishermen. They believe such activities should occur only when the game is needed for survival and no part of the animal is wasted.

Forests, deserts, and mountains are the typical arena for the adventuring Meistersinger. Rarely does a Meistersinger adventure anywhere unless animals are somehow involved —as mounts, as companions, or perhaps as captives who need to be set free.

Secondary Skills: Farmer, Forester, Groom, Hunter, Teamster/Freighter, Trapper/Furrier.

Weapon Proficiencies: The following weapons are forbidden to the Meistersinger: harpoon, lances, mancatcher, polearms, and trident.

As a hunter and woodsman, a Meistersinger must maintain a variety of weapons: those that are purely for melee, those that are purely missile weapons, and those that can be used in both melee and missile combat (hurled weapons). At 1st level, a Meistersinger must select one melee and one missile weapon. Each additional weapon proficiency slot must be spent in the following repetitive sequence: hurled, melee, missile.

Nonweapon Proficiencies: *Bonuses:* Animal Lore, Musical Instrument, Singing, Survival. *Suggested:* Agriculture, Animal Training, Blacksmithing, Craft Instrument, Dancing, Direction Sense, Fire-Building, Fish-ing, Herbalism, Hunting, Mountaineering, Riding (airborne), Riding (land-based), Rope Use, Set Snares, Swimming, Tracking, Weather Sense.

Armor/Equipment: Standard.

Special Benefits:

Song of Companionship: At 1st, 5th, and 10th levels, a Meistersinger can play the Song of Companionship, which lasts for 2d12 hours.

The DM and player should select six naturally occurring wild animals (not domesticated or fantasy-based) appropriate to the current terrain. A d6 is then rolled and the selected animal emerges from the nearby woods or over the next hill. The animal is a faithful companion to the Meistersinger from that day onward.

The Meistersinger and animal can communicate simple thoughts and desires. Such communication must be in the form of music or song by the Meistersinger, and a growl, caw, hiss, or some other appropriate sound by the animal. Others cannot understand the communication. The companion has hit points equal to those of the Meistersinger at his current level. The companion's hit points do not increase as the Meistersinger rises in level.

The companion gained at 1st level should be tiny or small (as per the "Size" entry in the *Monstrous Compendia*). The animal transfers its primary sensory power onto the Meistersinger. This is much like the *find familiar* spell, but it is not identical and does not take the place of that spell.

The 5th-level companion should be small or medium in size. The Meistersinger gains the ability to polymorph his arms and head into those of this companion, for purposes of unarmed combat. Attacks are made using the Meistersinger's THAC0, but successful attacks cause damage equal to that of the animal's natural weaponry. The Meistersinger also receives multiple attacks, if the animal is entitled to them.

The 10th-level companion should be medi-

um or large. The Meistersinger gains the ability to *shape change* (as the 9th-level wizard spell) into this companion's form once per day.

A Meistersinger's companions are his best friends. If one is slain, the mental strain of the loss forces the Meistersinger to roll a successful system shock check or die. (Likewise, if the Meistersinger is slain, the companion animals must roll system shock checks, at 80% + 1% per hit die.) If the check is successful, the Meistersinger goes into deep mourning for 101 days, during which he does not adventure. A Meistersinger can call for one replacement companion each time he advances in level (he is not required to call for a replacement). The replacement is the same size as the lost companion and confers the same abilities upon the Meistersinger.

Song of Sanction: This song envelops the Meistersinger, creating a nearly magical barri-
er of good will around him. Any attacking animal or monster must roll a saving throw vs. paralyzation with a −1 penalty per three levels of the Meistersinger or ignore the Meistersinger and those within one foot per level of him for as long as the song is played. The effect of the song is ended if the Meistersinger attempts to move or if anyone in the protected area attacks (including offensive spell use).

Animal Charm: Meistersingers know a number of songs that have special charm-like effects upon animals (including giant animals).

If the Meistersinger concentrates, he can attempt to charm one animal within view by his singing. Only an animal of Hit Dice equal to or less than the Meistersinger's level can be affected. Furthermore, the total Hit Dice of all such charmed animals accompanying the Meistersinger cannot exceed twice the Meistersinger's level.

The song takes 1d10 rounds, but the animal is held temporarily spellbound during the performance, as long as no hostile advances are made upon it by the Meistersinger or his allies. After 1d10 rounds, the monster rolls a saving throw vs. paralyzation with a −1 penalty per three levels of the Meistersinger. If it fails, it is under the effects of a *charm* spell. If it succeeds, it is unaffected and acts normally. If the roll was a natural 20, the animal is enraged and immediately attacks the Meistersinger.

Influence Reactions: Meistersingers can attempt to influence the reactions of animals that aren't attacking and that allow the Meistersinger to play for them. This ability is handled exactly as the True Bard's influence reactions ability (except that it affects only animals).

Special Hindrances: Meistersingers do not gain followers, nor do they build typical strongholds. Their animal companions serve as their followers, and they tend to build several small cottages or huts throughout the lands they patrol.

Riddlemaster

Specialty: Riddler/Intellect.

Qualifications: Riddlemasters must have an Intelligence of 15 or more. Their other ability scores are standard. Gnomes can rise to become 8th-level Riddlemasters. Halflings can advance up to 9th level.

Introduction: *Yes, I am Retean, the Riddlemaster, mastermind of enigmas and games. I can solve any riddle and complete any puzzle. Pay the price and watch me twice.*

As a Riddlemaster, my mind is constantly in motion. I'm wiser than most clerics, and smarter than most sages. Always thinking, always plotting, always alert.

*When I encounter someone, I analyze him, evaluate his value to myself, and act accordingly. When I enter a tavern I don't just grab the nearest chair. Instead, I scan the room, se-*lect *the most advantageous seat, and then evaluate the fare as I decide what to have. None of my decisions are made without deliberate, conscious thought.*

Yet, I can be entertaining as well. I love to pose questions and riddles. For example:

If the world were round,
And you stood on the ground,
How many places could you stand . . .
Walk south 20 leagues, east 20 leagues, north 20 leagues
and end up hand in hand.

The answer is not the north pole, but an infinite number of locations. Any point on a global ring lying 20 leagues north of a circle of latitude that divides evenly by 20 will work just fine.

And now, as I have summed up your worth to me, I must be off to a new challenge.

Description: Riddles, rhymes, and puzzles are the medium of the Riddlemaster. These characters look upon life as an intricate and challenging puzzle to be solved. Their seemingly strange ways cause many a commoner to label them crazy (much like the Jester). However, Riddlemasters are exceptionally intelligent, and their minds work on a level above that of the common man.

Riddlemasters devote their entire intellect to maximizing favorable outcomes for themselves and their friends. Some believe that Riddlemasters are just extraordinarily lucky, but this is not the case. Riddlemasters are always considering the environment around them, being sure to stand in the most favorable places, socializing with the most advantageous people, asking the best questions, and so on. They seek to develop the supreme mind.

To flaunt their skills, Riddlemasters often speak in riddles or rhymes, causing others to stop and think in order to understand them. Riddlemasters love to pose questions, in the form of riddles, to everyday people. These riddles are carefully constructed and often conceal lessons or observations that apply to the Riddlemasters' audience.

Role: Each Riddlemaster applies his intellect in a different way. Evil Riddlemasters seek to demean and put down others in order to rise above them. Good Riddlemasters make their way through society attempting to educate the "less fortunate." Others simply travel around, enjoying the sport of poking fun at others while advancing their own intellectual understanding.

Traveling Riddlemasters are most common, as their unique ways often irritate others, forcing them to maintain a mobile lifestyle. Adventuring Riddlemasters enjoy the supreme tests of judgment and intelligence that must be passed in order to survive perilous quests. Besides this, their input on decisions is nearly invaluable. Of course, some party members may find their manner difficult to put up with.

Secondary Skills: Few Riddlemasters have a secondary skill, as they have spent their time in intellectual pursuits. Those who do are most likely Gamblers, Jewelers, or Trader/Barterers.

Weapon Proficiencies: Riddlemasters enjoy finesse weapons over those that require simple brawn. They can become proficient in the blowgun, bow, crossbow, dagger, dart, hand axe, javelin, knife, quarterstaff, sling, spear, staff sling, short sword, or whip.

Nonweapon Proficiencies: *Bonuses:* Artistic Ability (riddles), Languages (modern), Poetry, Reading/Writing. *Suggested:* Appraising, Blind-fighting, Direction Sense, Gaming, Heraldry, Musical Instrument, Navigation, Reading Lips, Singing, Weather Sense, Ventriloquism.

Armor/Equipment: Standard.

Special Benefits:

Probable Path: Riddlemasters can use their great intellects to make analytical decisions. When a decision must be made concerning multiple options (*e.g.*, which hallway to proceed down, which door to open first, which opponent to attack first in order to achieve some goal, *etc.*), the Riddlemaster can use his intellect to help make the decision. In such cases, the DM secretly rolls an Intelligence check for the Riddlemaster, with a penalty equal to the number of previous probable path decisions made that day (representing mental fatigue). If the roll succeeds, the DM tells the player all significant clues that the Riddlemaster might know or observe. If there are no clues, no information is gained—Riddlemasters aren't lucky, they're just very intelligent.

If the roll is a natural 20, the information gained is misleading.

Unless a given situation changes somehow, using this ability multiple times in the same situation gives identical results.

Riddles/Puzzles: If any adventure includes an actual riddle or puzzle that the players must solve, the player of the Riddlemaster can make twice as many attempts to solve the riddle or puzzle as is normally allowed. For example, an adventure might include an

encounter in which the party runs into a sphinx. The sphinx may demand the answer to a riddle in exchange for safe passage. In this situation, if the Riddlemaster gives the answer, the player can actually make two guesses, and if either is correct, the sphinx is satisfied.

The same thing applies if the party comes across a room with a tiled floor that must be crossed in a specific sequence. The Riddlemaster is allowed to make one free mistake. Only on his second mistake does the character suffer any hazardous consequences.

If a problem has a time limit, the Riddlemaster has twice the allotted time to solve it.

A special use of solving riddles and puzzles occurs when a Riddlemaster attempts to understand a newly discovered spell. The Riddlemaster has a +10% bonus to his roll to learn spells (to a maximum of 95%).

Furthermore, the Riddlemaster gains the ability to use any written magical item at 8th level, instead of 10th level.

Common Sense: To signify the common sense a Riddlemaster has at his disposal, Riddlemasters gain certain benefits. Although these benefits are similar to those of the Jester kit, they are not luck, but rather a result of intellectual calculations made by the Riddlemaster.

• The Riddlemaster has a +1 adjustment to his Armor Class.

• A Riddlemaster receives a +1 (or 5%) bonus to many die rolls, including saving throws, individual initiative, attacks rolls, damage rolls, proficiency checks, thief skill checks, ability checks, and all ability-based rolls (bend bards, system shock, *etc.*), except for resurrection survival.

The only die rolls that common sense doesn't affect are surprise, initial character generation rolls, hit die rolls, resurrection sur-

vival, and monster damage rolls.

Riddling and Rhyming: By chanting certain riddles and rhymes, a Riddlemaster can influence an audience's reactions. This ability functions in all ways as the True Bard's influence reactions ability.

Special Hindrances: None.

Skald

Specialty: Viking Poet/Warrior.
Qualifications: Standard ability scores. Dwarves can advance up to the 12th level as Skalds.

Introduction:

I'm Herak the Skald
and I am quite bald,
but I have lots of gold,
as I am quite bold.

It needs a little work, but I can get to that latter. Welcome! Come in by the fire and I'll tell you a bit about my clan.

Being a Viking, I'm a great warrior and belong to the mightiest clan of raiders ever assembled. When we go on our great forays, it is I, Herak, who records our deeds for all to hear. But that is only part of my role as a Skald. When combat is fierce, I often chant one of the great war songs of my forefathers. These songs have great power, and more than once have I turned the tide of battle in our favor.

When my clan isn't at war or on a raid, I work on ballads, poems, and chants. It is our tradition that the clan's elder Skald pass on those songs that establish the clan's worth to the upcoming Skalds. To these are added the greatest tales of the current clansmen. In this way, all our descendants will know how great they are. They can retell these tales, sing the ballads, and thus establish their place among the clans.

Being a Skald is a wonderful life. There is nothing to match rowing a longboat across a mist-shrouded bay early in the morning, in preparation for a raid on some enemy village.

Everyone is silent, the only sound is the creaking of oars and soft slap of the water, and you can hear the chatter of teeth due to the cold and nerves. We eventually slip up onto land, enter the village, then I shout out a mighty chant and the fun begins.

Description: Skalds are honored and respected members of their clans. These great poets memorize the feats of each raid and battle, setting them down in the form of poetry.

Every war party loves to have a Skald in its midst. This assures that their great deeds and mighty skills will be honored in the Skald's next recital, and thereafter immortalized for all time. Members of most bands treat Skalds with utmost respect and courtesy. It is well known that the foolish warrior who maligns a Skald will soon hear his name slandered in innumerable ballads across the land.

Poems are the form in which Skalds honor others and themselves. Poems are also used to relate the oral history of the clan. Significant ballads are passed down from one generation to another via the Skald's talents. In this way, the lessons and deeds of the past are related to those of the present so they can be passed into the future.

Role: Skalds are often supported and protected by clan nobles and kings who love to hear of great duels and mighty wars. When events are unfolded in the form of poetry, it makes the telling all the more inspiring. Such men would hear Skalds relate tales of their family's glory to visitors.

Skalds rarely perform together unless they have entered into a poetic duel.

Adventuring Skalds are common. Every Skald is easily caught up in the fervor and majesty of adventure, danger, and combat. Great quests also serve as source material for their ballads and poems.

Secondary Skills: Armorer, Bowyer/Fletcher, Hunter, Leather worker, Weaponsmith.

Weapon Proficiencies: An initial proficiency slot must be spent on either the broad

sword, hand axe, battle axe, or spear. At least half of the Skald's weapon proficiencies must be spent on these weapons (until they are all selected).

Nonweapon Proficiencies: *Bonuses:* Ancient History, Local History, Poetry, Singing. *Suggested:* Armorer, Blacksmithing, Blindfighting, Bowyer/Fletcher, Crowd Working, Etiquette, Hunting, Leatherworking, Musical Instrument, Weaponsmithing.

See "Special Hindrances" concerning the reading/writing proficiency.

Armor/Equipment: Skalds lean toward warrior skills more than most bards. Because of this, they can wear any form of armor up to bronze plate, and they can even use shields.

Special Benefits:

War Chant: By chanting a war song, a Skald can inspire allies as they go forward into combat. For the chant to have an effect, the Skald must begin chanting at least three rounds before combat begins, otherwise his allies are too caught up in the events about them to benefit from this ability.

Such chanting has an effective range of ten feet per level of the Skald. The effects end as soon as the Skald receives his first wound. If the Skald does not enter the fray (and avoids being wounded), the effects end in a number of rounds equal to the Skald's level.

At 1st level, the Skald can choose only one of the following six effects per battle; at 3rd level two effects are chosen, three at 6th, four at 9th, *etc.* The Skald player chooses the effects, and can change them from one battle to the next.

Chanting can elevate spirits, remove concerns about danger, keep men's minds focused on combat, and fill friendly forces with a sense of being larger than life. Translated into game terms, this results in the following six possible effects for the members of the Skald's party:

• Bonus hit points equal to the Skald's Hit Dice.

• A morale bonus of 1 for every six levels

of the Skald (rounded up).

• A +1 bonus to all attack rolls.
• A +1 bonus to all damage rolls.
• A +1 bonus to all saving throws.
• A −1 bonus to everyone's Armor Class.

Influence Reactions: If a Skald spends 1d10 rounds singing ballads, he can attempt to improve the reactions of an audience. Everyone able to clearly hear and understand the Skald must roll a saving throw vs. paralyzation with a −1 penalty per three levels of the Skald. Those who fail have their reactions to the Skald improved by one level. Those who succeed do not find the Skald's ballad to be particularly moving. Those who succeed on a natural 20 find the song to be offensive and their reactions worsen one level.

Battle Chant: Skalds are a bit more combative than most bards. This provides them with certain combat advantages. The Skald fights

with a +1 attack roll bonus any time he is singing or chanting during combat, even a soft chant under his breath. In addition, the Skald gains a +1 damage bonus when using a broadsword, axe (any type), or spear while he is chanting, provided that he has proficiency with the weapon. These bonuses almost always apply, unless the bard is silenced, underwater, *etc.*

Legend Lore: Skalds love legends about war and combat. Legend lore works the same for Skalds as it does for True Bards, except that Skalds can perform legend lore only upon magical items having to do with war or combat (*e.g.*, weapons, armor, *strength potions,* etc.).

Special Hindrances: The Skald's society does not have a written language. Because of this, Skalds cannot take the reading/writing proficiency when created. Furthermore, they do not get the read languages ability at 3rd level if they stay in their home society. However, both of these limits are lifted once the Skald comes into contact with a culture that reads and writes. He can then pick up the reading/writing proficiency at twice the normal cost and gains the read languages ability at a 0% base (*i.e.*, he must put points into the skill or he has a zero chance for success).

Skalds do not gain the use any written magical item ability at 10th level.

Spells are also nearly unknown in the Skald's society, and they are viewed with suspicion in any event. Thus, Skalds cannot learn any spells until they encounter a spellcasting culture. Once contact has been made, the Skald can begin casting spells when he gains his next level. At this time he is considered a 2nd-level spellcaster (providing he is at least 3rd level by this time). His spellcasting level increases by 1 every time he gains a level thereafter.

If your campaign does not have a Viking culture, but a player still wishes to play a Skald, assume that the character left his distant homeland and has journeyed to the existing campaign setting. This character can take reading/writing proficiency when he gains his next level, provided he has the proficiency slots available. He gains the ability to cast spells as outlined above.

Notes: The *Vikings Campaign Sourcebook* is a good resource to be used in conjunction with Skald bards.

Thespian

Specialty: Actor/Mime.
Qualifications: Standard ability scores.
Introduction: *I am Glateela the Thespian. I would like to invite you to the performance of the "Green Dragon and Golden Knight," given this weeks' end in the Old King's Theater. I will be playing Maiden Zephnia.*

I have played various roles on the Old King's stage for the past four years. Acting is a wonderful occupation. I'm always busy learning parts, performing, and teaching the young children. When I'm not performing, some courtly gentleman or other has me over for blackroot tea. I'm on a first-name basis with the city mayor, all of the ranking constables, and even the Duke knows me.

What few people realize is that I'm sister to the infamous wanderer Hanalacious, and we often adventure together. Hanalacious is actually a warrior. Her reputation as a bard is a result of my dressing up as her double and acting the part. In this way, the legend of Hanalacious grows with a speed that would be impossible for any single human.

Unknown even to Hana is the fact that I occasionally play other off-stage roles. This is the real thrill of being a Thespian. You can be anyone you want if you are good enough.

Hope to see you this weekend. And if you whisper a word of my secret to anyone, you'd best beware of everyone you meet, for one of them will be me in disguise and I will silence your loose tongue forever.

Description: Of all the various types of bards, Thespians put the most time and en-

ergy into performances. Thespians are actors. They display their talents in plays, skits, and dramatic productions. Some even perform in streets or village squares. When a Thespian isn't acting, he is likely writing scripts or reading for upcoming parts.

Thespians are somewhat like, yet unlike, Charlatans. Where Charlatans act to deceive, Thespians act to make others believe. Because of their similar methods, Thespians have some skills in common with Charlatans.

Role: Thespians rarely travel from town to town unless they are on an acting tour. Even if they are on tour, they often return to their established home. Most Thespians belong to the local actor's guild and take part in regularly scheduled performances.

Occasionally, Thespians are secretly hired to serve as spies, or temporarily fill in for a missing person. The great Thespian Hanalacious once filled in as the Lord Mayor of the Free City of Greyhawk for over a month while the real mayor was away on secret errands.

The adventuring Thespian is a rare person (player characters represent almost all of them). Such Thespians are often out for "field research." After all, if you want to play the part of a mighty warrior, what better practice than to go dungeoneering? Other Thespians adventure for the thrill of it all. They look upon such activity as taking a part in the "Grand Play of Life." Such Thespians often go to any length to mold the adventure into a dramatic production with themselves as the stars—often to the chagrin of their fellow party members.

Secondary Skills: Any.

Weapon Proficiencies: Since they are actors, Thespians spend a lot of time practicing with all types of weapons, in order to make their plays more realistic. This produces a unique situation. Thespians understand the showy stage methods for using most weapons, but they rarely practice with any one weapon long enough to become truly proficient at it.

As a result, 1st-level Thespians are proficient only with the dagger. At 2nd level they become proficient with the knife, and at 5th level Thespians gain their final weapon proficiency—the short sword.

This restriction is partially offset by the fact that a Thespian suffers only a −2 nonproficiency penalty (equal to that of warriors) on all other weapons because of practicing with these weapons during rehearsals.

Nonweapon Proficiencies: *Bonuses:* Acting, Disguise, Languages (modern), Reading/Writing. *Suggested:* Artistic Ability, Crowd Working, Dancing, Etiquette, Jumping, Languages (ancient), Musical Instrument, Poetry, Reading Lips, Seamstress/Tailor, Singing, Tumbling, Ventriloquism, Weaving.

Armor/Equipment: Again, Thespians are actors and don all forms of armor for their various roles. This sets them apart from the norm. As a result, they can wear any form of

armor and even carry shields. However, they incur a +1 Armor Class penalty when wearing armor that is not standard for the bard character class (their understanding of these armor types is imperfect). Thespians have no real understanding of shields; though they can carry shields, they gain no Armor Class bonus for the effort.

Special Benefits:

General Acting: Thespians are masterful actors. Using this ability, they can act as if a light blow was fatal, pretend to faint, or exaggerate their abilities. These skills are required on stage, but are also very useful during adventures.

Once, Hanalacious's band came upon a camp of six ogres. Realizing that they were outmatched, Hana leapt forward to meet the charging ogres. She acted as if the first strike against her was a fatal blow. The ogres believed this and charged on to attack the rest of the band. With the time that Hana had bought herself, she managed to unpack her *fireball* scroll and succeeded in roasting the ogres and saving the day.

Hana's finest performance occurred in the famous dungeons of the Greyhawk ruins. Here, she came upon Farcluun, a great red dragon. During the next four hours, Hanalacious was involved in the most dangerous role she ever played. When she saw the great wyrm, she quickly disguised herself as Zagig Yragerne, the original founder of Greyhawk Castle. Entering the cavern of Farcluun, Hana played up her knowledge, wisdom, and magical prowess. In the end, she cowed Farcluun and actually had the dragon huddled in a corner with threats of turning its life's treasure trove into an ant hill.

Acting functions in much the same way as illusion spells. If the audience believes the act, then it works without question. If the audience is skeptical, they are allowed to roll a saving throw vs. spell with a −1 penalty for every three levels of the Thespian. If the saving throw succeeds, they realize that the Thespian is acting; otherwise, they accept the act.

Of course, acts can go only so far. It is impossible to act as if you are lifting a 700-pound boulder over your head unless you have the aid of magic (or a Strength of 20 or more).

Spell Acting: Any Thespian who has taken the spellcraft proficiency can act as if he can cast powerful spells. To put on such a performance, the Thespian must be easily viewed by all who will be affected. The Thespian then stands up, chants arcane words, gestures, and tosses "magical" powder about. During the spell acting, the Thespian directs his attention and gestures toward the intended targets of the spell. After one round, the targets must roll a successful morale check or flee in terror.

If the Thespian actually casts a flashy spell during the act (*e.g., burning hands*), the morale check is made with a penalty equal to the spell's level. Imagine what you would think if a wizard's hands sprouted flame while he chanted and made gestures of doom in your direction.

Influence Reactions: Thespians can influence the reactions of those they meet by trying to act in an appealing manner. After 1d10 rounds of such a performance, those associating with the Thespian roll a saving throw vs. paralyzation with a −1 penalty per three levels of the Thespian. If they fail the saving throw, their initial reactions are altered one level in the direction that the Thespian desires. If the saving throw succeeds, the audience realizes that the Thespian is acting and their reactions are adjusted one level in the opposite direction.

Observe Motions: As actors, Thespians are trained to observe the motions of others. Usually they use this skill to see cues from fellow actors during a performance. This ability also enables them to predict the movements of opponents during combat.

In any round that a Thespian wins initiative, he gains a +2 bonus to his Armor Class and saving throws and a +1 bonus to attack rolls.

Special Hindrances: None.

Creating New Kits

Although the list of kits given in this handbook is large, it isn't all-inclusive. There are many other bard kits that DMs and players can come up with.

Before designing a new kit, first examine the existing kits to see if one of them can be modified to fill your needs. If not, make a photocopy of the Bard Kit Record Sheet located in the back of this handbook. Fill it out with the description of your new kit. The information that should be listed under each section is described in detail at the beginning of this chapter. Refer to it for assistance.

After you have created a new kit, present it to your Dungeon Master for approval. Often, he will wish to adjust certain aspects of the new kit for balance. Once the kit is complete and ready for use, the Dungeon Master still might adjust it in the future, based on how well it works in play.

Here is a helpful list of additional bard kits that you may wish to create on your own.

- Historical Bard—Druid historian
- Dervish—Arabian Dancer/Healer
- Muse—Singing Healer
- Scop—Anglo-Saxon Minstrel
- Entrancer—Spell Dancer
- Troubadour—Thief/Illusionist
- Poet—Courtier/Romeo
- Rustic—Folk Singer
- Rhythmist—Instrumental Dancer
- Savage—Medicine Man
- Sleuth—Spy
- Legionnaire—Cavalier

Acquiring, Dropping, and Changing Kits

Bard kits should be taken only when the character is first created. The one exception might occur when this handbook is first introduced into a campaign. In this case, the Dungeon Master may allow certain existing bards to be converted to the kits that most resemble the manner in which they have been played in the past. However, note that such a transfer will have to be adjudicated by the Dungeon Master.

If a player decides to drop a bard kit, he should meet with his Dungeon Master to discuss the manner in which the transition should occur. When a kit is dropped, the character becomes a core bard (not a True Bard), and that character cannot regain his old kit. This has the following effects upon the character:

- Future weapon proficiency slots can be spent on any weapon desired.
- The bard's four bonus proficiencies must either be dropped or all future nonweapon proficiency slots must be spent paying for them before any new nonweapon proficiencies can be selected.
- The character no longer needs to pay attention to his old kit's suggested nonweapon proficiencies.
- The character can wear any armor normally allowed to the core bard, but cannot use any other type of armor (including shields).
- All special benefits are lost.
- All special hindrances are ignored.

It is possible for a bard to change kits, but only in one very limited manner. First, the bard's existing kit must be dropped. Then, if the bard wants, he may gain a new kit, but it must be the True Bard kit. The process for gaining the True Bard kit goes as follows.

- Once the bard's old bonus nonweapon proficiencies are either dropped or paid for, the next available proficiency slots must be spent gaining singing, musical instrument, reading/writing (native tongue), and local history.
- As the bard gains the next four levels, he gains one of the True Bard's special benefits at each new level. The specific benefit gained is determined by the player.

Demi-, Multi-, and Dual-Classed Bards

Demihumans as Bards

As per the *Player's Handbook*, only humans and half-elves can become bards. Even this book doesn't allow dwarves, elves, gnomes, and halflings to become bards in the true sense of the word. However, each of these races has a strong tradition in the performing arts. Dwarven chanters are legendary, as are the great elven minstrels. Gnome professors and halfling whistlers are also well-known.

Unlike humans and half-elves, those playing demihumans must take a bard kit if they are to run bard player characters. If the kit system is not used, dwarves, elves, gnomes, and halflings cannot be bards. Since these races cannot be true bards, they are referred to as demi-bards. Only a few kits are open to these races, but each race has a kit that is available only to members of that race (indicated by *italic* type in the following table).

Table 13: DEMI-BARDS

Race Kit	Maximum Level
Dwarves*	
Chanter	15
Herald	6
Skald	12
Elves	
Gypsy	9
Herald	6
Loremaster	12
Meistersinger	15
Minstrel	15
Gnomes**	
Charlatan	6
Herald	6
Professor	15
Jester	15
Jongleur	9
Riddlemaster	8
Halflings*	
Herald	6
Jester	8
Jongleur	12
Riddlemaster	9
Whistler	15

Counter Spell: Dwarves and halflings are extremely nonmagical. These two demi-bards are not allowed to cast spells. They also fail to receive the 10th-level bard ability to use any written magical item.

However, as demi-bards, these two races possess the curiosity of all bards. This leads them to study the workings of magic (*i.e.*, dwarf and halfling demi-bards must take the spellcraft proficiency). Although this doesn't result in the acquisition of magical powers, it enables them to gain special resistances to spells they understand.

If a halfling or dwarf is able to find a spell and learn it (*i.e.*, succeed with their "chance to learn spells" roll), they become highly resistant to the effects of that spell. Of course, these two races can learn to resist only spells of the same level as bards are typically able to cast. Thus, a 2nd-level dwarf or halfling demi-bard can learn how to resist the effects of all 1st-level spells that he has learned (as per Table 6: Spell Progression). Of course, the demi-bard is still limited to the number of spells he can learn to counter. This limit is set by his "Maximum # of Spells per level" (an aspect of Intelligence).

When a dwarf or halfling demi-bard is subjected to a learned spell's effects, he can roll his "chance to learn spells" in an attempt to thwart the spell's effects. This roll is in addition to all other saving throws normally allowed. This does not cancel the spell; it simply prevents it from having any effect upon the dwarf or halfling demi-bard.

**Illusions:* Gnomes have a hard time understanding and casting the more practical and substantial spells. They prefer spells that

create illusions, flashy colors, and other wondrous effects. Because of this, gnome demibards do not gain the full range of spells normally allowed to bards. Instead, they must select and use spells as if they were illusionists. However, they still use Table 6: Spell Progression, to determine the number of spells they cast at a given level.

Demihuman Kits

Following are four kits available only to demihumans. These kits cannot be selected by humans. However, half-elves can select the Minstrel kit, advancing up to 12th level.

Dwarven Chanter

Specialty: Chanter/Time Lord.

Qualifications: Chanters must have a Constitution of 13 or more. However, they have no Intelligence qualification (unlike most bards). Only dwarves can become Chanters and they are limited to 15th level in advancement.

Description: Many times have other races attempted to analyze the phenomenal success of the dwarven race; their uncanny ability to survive incredible hardship, their dogged nature, the immense amount of work they perform, and their successful military campaigns. Always the analysis comes up short.

Much of the success of the dwarven race can be attributed to their Chanters. Throughout the ages, these special dwarves have passed along the secrets of their kind. They have learned the many mining, forging, marching, and war chants of their elders. Other races dismiss these chants as simple entertainment, but it is the power of the dwarven Chanter that has built the steel in the dwarven spine. If a skilled Chanter is present, dwarves can mine through solid granite for months without growing bored or lax.

Some chants are purely vocal, but many require the use of a percussion instrument to keep the rhythm steady. Chanters often employ drums, gongs, gourds, and so on.

Role: The secret of chanting has been kept hidden from outsiders. Thus, Chanters are heavily guarded and highly regarded within the dwarven kingdom. Of all dwarven organizations, the Chanter's College is one of the most powerful. Even kings have been overruled in the past by mighty Chanters threatening to cease their rhythmic songs. Without the Chanters, the dwarven communities would slow to a crawl and their underworld enemies would push them from their homes.

Adventuring Chanters are a great boon to any party and are even more useful in large-scale battles. They are the pace-setters and the very heartbeat of those around them.

Secondary Skills: Armorer, Jeweler, Mason, Miner, Weaponsmith.

Weapon Proficiencies: Chanters often use their weapons to beat upon an instrument, a rock, or even the ground. Because of this, they generally become proficient only in blunt weapons or stick-like weapons.

The following weapons are available to Chanters: club, flails (all), maces (all), javelin, morning star, quarterstaff, sling, spear, staff sling, and the warhammer.

Nonweapon Proficiencies: *Bonuses:* Crowd Working, Musical Instrument, Chanting, Spellcraft. *Suggested:* Ancient History, Appraising, Armorer, Blacksmithing, Cobbling, Craft Instrument, Engineering, Gem Cutting, Languages (ancient), Languages (modern), Local History, Mining, Mountaineering, Pottery, Stonemasonry, Weaponsmithing.

Armor/Equipment: Chanters can wear any armor except for plate; plate mail, bronze plate, field plate, and full plate are all forbidden. They cannot employ shields.

Special Benefits:

Counter Chant: Like all dwarven demibards, dwarven Chanters gain the counter spell ability defined earlier. In order to counter a spell, a Chanter must voice the proper counter chant.

In addition to the typical counter spell ability, Chanters can actually "attack" certain spells. A Chanter can walk up to a wall of force (assuming he has previously learned the spell), begin counter chanting, and if he succeeds with his "chance to learn spells" roll, he actually cancels the entire spell for a number of rounds equal to his level. If the roll is equal to or less than the dwarf's level, the cancellation is permanent.

War Chant: Dwarven war chants are legendary. There is nothing quite so powerful and terrifying as watching a mass of heavily armed and grim-looking dwarves advancing and chanting. Their deep voices, all booming in unison, often destroy enemy morale and put fear into the heart of many a brave foe.

When a Chanter starts a war chant, he can affect up to ten dwarves per level or one non-dwarf per level. To be affected, the recipients must join in the chant (it doesn't matter if they have ever heard it or not). After 1d10 rounds of chanting, the power of the chant begins to take effect. A chanting band gains a +1 bonus to initiative, a +2 bonus to resist surprise, and a +2 bonus to all morale checks. Those combating a chanting group suffer a −1 initiative penalty and a −2 penalty to all morale checks. The bonuses for a member of the Chanter's party last for as long as both the individual and the Chanter are chanting; the penalties for the opponents last as long as the Chanter keeps up the chant.

Timing Chant: The real power of the Chanter is the numerous timing chants he knows. These chants function similarly to war chants in that they take 1d10 rounds to take effect, and last while both the Chanter and affected are chanting. But the results are quite different.

There are four common timing chants: one each for mining, forging, marching, and general labor. The purpose of each chant is to increase productivity, soothe the mind, prevent boredom, stave off sleep, and support resolve. All timing chants must be accompanied by a percussion instrument.

Timing chants by Chanters increase speed or production by 5% per level of the Chanter. A top-level (15th) Chanter can get 75% more work out of a group than it would normally produce.

Of course, such rapid work does take a physical toll, even if the mind is willing. Each hour that a person works under the effects of a timing chant, he must roll a Constitution check. A failed check results in the loss of 1d4 hit points. This damage is temporary and is recoverable at the rate of 1 point per hour of rest or sleep. Anyone reduced to 0 hit points in this way falls over from exhaustion; death results unless a Constitution check succeeds.

Trance: Obviously, if a mining crew's Chanter falls over from lack of sleep or exhaustion, the timing chant will cease. For this reason, Chanters have learned to place themselves into a self-induced trance. This takes 1d10 turns of uninterrupted meditation, during which the Chanter grumbles the words to some ancient meditative script. Once in a trance state, the Chanter will begin some set activity: chanting, combat, marching, working, studying, *etc.*

The trance state causes the Chanter to shut down all of his being (mind and body) that is not needed for the activity at hand. An entranced Chanter can maintain this set activity until a predetermined circumstance occurs. For example, the Chanter may have said to himself, "Awake when there are no more goblins on the field of battle," "Awake when we reach the Kingdom of Thorbardin," or "Awake after 1,000 strikes of the great drum."

Trances are not lightly entered, as they are very dangerous to the character. During a trance state, the Chanter does not drink, eat, rest, or sleep. Every time that one of these activities should normally occur, the entranced Chanter must roll a Constitution check. A failed check results in the loss of hit points: 1d8 for drink, 1d3 for food, 1d4 for rest, and 1d8 for sleep. Furthermore, the only known

way to interrupt a trance before the predetermined circumstance occurs is to reduce the Chanter to 0 hit points (*i.e.*, knock him unconscious or kill him).

Damage resulting from food and water deprivation must be healed as if it were combat damage, but damage resulting from lack of rest or sleep is temporary and can be regained at the rate of 1 point per hour of rest or sleep. If reduced to 0 hit points by sleep or rest deprivation, the entranced Chanter falls unconscious; death results unless a Constitution check succeeds. However, if all damage is a result of food and water deprivation, the Chanter dies regardless of the check result.

Special Hindrances: Like all dwarven demibards, Chanters do not gain the bard's spell abilities. Nor do they gain the 10th-level bard ability to use any written magical item.

Elven Minstrel

Specialty: Elven Spell Singer.

Qualifications: Only elves and half-elves can become Minstrels. Elves can advance up to 15th level as Minstrels, while half-elves are limited to 12th level.

Description: Of all musicians in the world, none can play as purely as an elf. Minstrels spend their entire lives seeking musical perfection. Of course, the definition of perfection differs from one culture to the next. Elves believe that music should be simple, pure, beautiful, and natural. Furthermore, those who listen should become lost in the music, and their spirits should transcend their bodies to ride upon the sweet flow of glittering notes.

Elves are a very magical race, and this is especially true of Minstrels. It is said that Minstrels cast spells by the simple strumming of an instrument.

Role: Within elven society, Minstrels are regarded as nobles. Minstrel groups perform during annual festivals for the enjoyment of all, and kings invite them to dine in exchange for an evening's song. Outside their own culture, elven Minstrels are looked upon with envy, distrust, and some fear.

Elven Minstrels occasionally adventure out into the world. Some seek life-experience to heighten the quality of their music. Others simply wander, relishing the sensation of freedom that inspires their songs. A few Minstrels seek to purge themselves of some impure act or event.

Secondary Skills: Minstrels train to be great musicians all their lives. They do not spend the time necessary to learn a secondary skill. Thus, Minstrels have no secondary skills.

Weapon Proficiencies: Elven Minstrels are limited to the following weapon proficiencies: blowgun, bow (any), dagger, dart, hand axe, javelin, knife, quarterstaff, sling, spear, staff sling, long and short swords, and the trident.

Nonweapon Proficiencies: *Bonuses:* Musical Instrument, Reading/Writing, Singing, Spellcraft. *Suggested:* Ancient History, Artistic Ability, Craft Instrument, Etiquette, Heraldry, Local History, Poetry.

Armor/Equipment: Minstrels can wear only leather armor, padded armor, or elven chain mail. Even studded leather is considered too harsh for a Minstrel to don.

Special Benefits:

Special Resistance: Elven Minstrels gain a +2 saving throw bonus against all magical effects based on music. If the attack does not allow a saving throw, they receive a normal saving throw, anyway.

Spell Singing: Minstrels are some of the few beings still in existence who know the ancient art of spell singing. Some sages claim that magic was originally released into the Prime Material plane by an ancient master musician. These sages maintain that music is the true catalyst for ultimate sorcery. Whether this is true or not, it is a fact that elven Minstrels cast spells through their music.

Minstrels cannot cast spells in the typical manner. When a spell calls for a somatic component, they must play an instrument. Likewise, they must sing when a spell requires a verbal component.

Material components must be carried on the Minstrel's person in a specially prepared bag (made from deer leather). The Minstrel need not reach into the bag or manipulate the material components. When the spell is cast, the components simply vanish from within the bag. If the bag does not contain the required components, the spell does not function.

Not all instruments can be used for spell singing. First of all, if a spell requires a verbal component (singing), only those instruments that leave the Minstrel's mouth free can be used. This eliminates most of the wind instruments. If the spell requires a somatic component, the instrument must support numerous, complex hand manipulations (as is true of any stringed instrument). This eliminates gongs, cymbals, drums, and most of the percussion family. Thus, elven Minstrels typically carry stringed instruments. Keyboard instruments would work but are generally too bulky to carry around.

Spells that normally emanate from the caster's hands instead radiate from the spell singer's instrument. Thus, *burning hands* produces its 120-degree arc of flame from the instrument (and not the Minstrel's hands).

Spell singing is in all other ways just like typical spell casting.

Influence Reactions: This ability works just like the True Bard's ability of the same name. However, a Minstrel can sing or play an instrument in an attempt to influence reactions. And, if the Minstrel does both, he can adjust the reactions by two levels instead of the typical one. This is not cumulative with the crowd working proficiency or the bard's reputation.

Counter Song: The last special benefit of the Minstrel is identical to the True Bard's

counter song ability in every way.

Special Hindrances: Without an instrument, Minstrels cannot cast spells that require somatic components.

Gnome Professor

Specialty: Lecturer.

Qualifications: The standard qualifications for Intelligence and Charisma are switched for gnome Professors (*i.e.*, they must have a minimum Intelligence of 15 and Charisma of 13). Prime Requisites also change to Intelligence and Charisma. Only gnomes can become Professors, and they can advance up to 15th level.

Description: Professors are an odd sort; other races have a hard time deciding whether these strange gnomes are geniuses or fools. Half of their speeches and inventions seem revolutionary. The rest of their speeches sound like endless babbling, and most their in-

ventions are death traps that injure more gnomes than they help.

Professors are eccentric gnomes who love to tinker with things: chemicals, gears, pulleys, magic, and so on. For a Professor, gaining knowledge for its own sake is wasteful. Only when it is being used to develop "things of consequence" is knowledge worthwhile. Professors often say, "If the textbooks don't make sense, throw 'em away and approach the problem experimentally."

Above all, Professors feel that they have an obligation to educate the ignorant and provide them with mechanical wonders to help elevate their standard of living.

Role: Professors are held in high regard within gnome society. Every gnome loves to sit in on one of their frequent lectures or to have a Professor over for tea. Yet, when Professors get that odd glint in their eyes and start experimenting, even their brethren know to

run for their little lives.

Adventuring Professors are often intense and fanatically greedy for knowledge. Those who are dangerous threats to other gnomes are actively encouraged to go out and help "educate" the other races. But there are certain Professors who truly possess some small spark of genius within them. These Professors often realize the potential knowledge and practical experience that adventuring can provide, and they set out to explore the world.

Secondary Skills: Professors can have any secondary skill.

Weapon Proficiencies: Professors are very eccentric and love complex devices with multiple moving parts. This personality trait is evident in the type of weapons they select. Professors can become proficient in the following weapons: arquebus, blowgun, bow, crossbow, harpoon, mancatcher, scourge, sling, staff sling, and whip.

Nonweapon Proficiencies: *Bonuses:* Ancient History, Languages (ancient), Languages (modern), Reading/Writing. *Suggested:* Agriculture, Animal Lore, Appraising, Astrology, Brewing, Cooking, Direction Sense, Engineering, Etiquette, Fire-Building, Gem Cutting, Heraldry, Herbalism, Local History, Musical Instrument, Navigation, Religion, Rope Use, Spellcraft, Weather Sense, Whistling/Humming.

Armor/Equipment: Professors are not overly concerned about the practicality of wearing good armor. They tend to wear something comfortable unless they are experimenting with armor functionality.

Professors wear only leather, studded leather, or padded armor on a regular basis. However, each month, a Professor can experiment with one type of armor (even shields) for up to 1d10 days. When experimenting and wearing other armor, the Professor suffers a +1 Armor Class penalty and loses all Dexterity defense adjustments.

Special Benefits:

Legend Lore: This ability is exactly like the True Bard's ability of the same name.

Profess: All Professors give frequent speeches to anyone who will listen. Although this can be entertaining and occasionally educational, such lectures have little direct impact upon play. However, if a Professor is able to examine a situation and evaluate it, he sometimes comes up with a great plan. The act of revealing such a plan is known as "professing."

When a Professor examines a given situation for 1d10 rounds, he is able to determine several good plans to deal with the situation. If the Professor communicates (professes) this information to his comrades, and they heed the information, certain benefits result.

After professing a course of action, the Professor player is able to hand out a number of bonuses equal to the Professor's level. These bonuses can be applied to any die roll (prior to the roll) that the Professor designates, as long as the affected individual is following the Professor's suggested course of action. (If the roll is being made on percentage dice, the bonus is 5%, otherwise a +1 bonus results).

As an example, imagine that an adventuring party has spied through a keyhole into a room. The gnome Professor, Nowtal, asks if he can have a look. After examining the orc-infested room for six rounds (a 6 was rolled on the 1d10), Nowtal comes up with a plan. The player then role-plays his character, informing the other players of the plan: "Torcan, you slip around to the side door and jump into the room in an attempt to startle the orcs, then Larcon Heavy-Hand can charge the main door in hopes of breaking it down for a surprise rear attack. During the commotion, Lefty will slip over to that chest and attempt to make away with any interesting contents."

As the party proceeds with the plan, Nowtal's player hands out a +1 bonus on Torcan's attempt to surprise the orcs. He also boosts Larcon's bend bars attempt (to increase his chance to break down the bolted door by 5%). Since Nowtal is only 3rd level, he has only one more bonus to hand out. He could

use it to improve Larcon or Torcan's attack roll, increase damage, *etc.* Instead he gives it to the thief, Lefty. However, Lefty's player has decided to backstab an orc instead of dashing over to the chest. Thus, the DM rules that Lefty isn't following the Professor's plan and Nowtal's player will have to use his last bonus somewhere else. Just then, an orc shaman casts a fireball from a *necklace of missiles* and the last bonus is used to help Larcon with his saving throw.

Note that these bonuses last only for one die roll. These single bonuses cannot be combined into a +2 (10%) or better bonus.

Mechanically Inclined: Of all known devices, Professors love those with multiple moving parts more than any other.

Since Professors are mechanically inclined, they can find and remove traps. The chance to succeed at this progresses just as the "find/remove traps" skill on Table 19: Thief Average

Ability Table, in the *DMG*. Since Professors approach traps from a purely mechanical standpoint, they receive no racial, Dexterity, or armor adjustments to this roll.

This same percentage chance can be used to help solve other mechanical problems—much like having a "mechanical proficiency." For example, if the party comes upon a futuristic device, such as steam-driven bellows, the Professor can examine it in an attempt to understand how it works. If the roll succeeds, the DM should inform the player that his character understands the device. Through role-playing, the player can then tell the rest of the party how to operate it.

Invention: A Professor's most useful ability, and his most dangerous, is that of invention. Professors love to invent odd gadgets, such as sword hilts with screw-on blades that can be used as short, long, broad, bastard, or two-handed swords. Another invention might be a wagon pulled by draft horses located in the center of the wagon. This protects the animals from attack and allows the teamster to feed them as they walk.

A Professor's chance to succeed with an invention is based upon his "mechanical proficiency" (see previous paragraphs). From that base chance, the DM must assess the difficulty of an invention and apply a modifier (usually in the range of −25% to +25%). If the proper tools, raw materials, and time are available, a successful roll indicates that the invention works. If the roll is below the Professor's level, the invention is a great success. However, if the roll fails, the invention either has some major flaw or is a total flop. If the failed roll is a 95% or higher, the failure results in an injury, as determined by the Dungeon Master. A roll of 100 indicates that a fatality results unless the victim rolls a successful saving throw vs. paralyzation.

Special Hindrances: Unlike typical bards, gnomes are not eligible to learn and cast spells from any school of magic. Instead, they are restricted to the spell selection available to

illusionists. This is further explained in the "Illusion" note found earlier in the "Demi-Bard" section.

Halfling Whistler

Specialty: Wanderer.

Qualifications: Whistlers must have a Wisdom of 13 or better. However, qualifying Intelligence is lowered to 10. Prime requisites for Whistlers are Wisdom and Charisma.

Halflings are the only race able to become Whistlers. They are limited to 15th level.

Description: Much like dwarven Chanters, halfling Whistlers are the unheralded heroes of the halfling race. Halflings belong to the general category of nature-sensitive races and professions. Because halflings hate to kill forest animals for food or butcher farm pets, they live by using their knack for agriculture.

Their success is largely due to the existence of halfling Whistlers. Although almost any halfling can whistle up a tune, true Whistlers are extremely rare. Each halfling community has but one or two.

Whistlers are extremely attuned to the natural environment about them. In particular, they love forest animals and all types of plant life. The very tunes of a skilled Whistler can help a garden overcome drought or blight. Whistlers can also communicate with birds to help prevent insect swarms from wiping out a village's food supply.

When Whistlers aren't tending gardens and crops, they can be found performing for the locals. Nearly every day, a comfortable crowd forms in some grassy section of the community for an evening's entertainment. Some just sit on the grass and listen to the Whistlers' tunes, while others dance about, laugh, and make merry.

Role: Whistlers are an odd mix of a farmer, forest wanderer, and entertainer. Although they are loved by everyone in the community, most of them seem a bit reclusive, often living on the edge of town or even in a small burrow just within the forest's edge. In truth, they aren't reclusive—they are simply maintaining their unique link with nature.

Secondary Skills: Farmer, Forester, Fisher, Leather Worker, Tailor/Weaver, Trapper/Furrier (but see below).

Weapon Proficiencies: Like all halflings, Whistlers love missile weapons, particularly those that can be thrown. At least half of a Whistler's weapons must be types that can be hurled.

Whistlers can select from among the following weapons: blowgun, short bow (either type), club, light crossbow, dagger, dart, footman's mace, hand axe, harpoon, javelin, knife, quarterstaff, sling, spear, staff sling, short sword, or war hammer.

In addition to these, Whistlers can take a special weapon proficiency: rock pitching. All halflings are skilled at pitching rocks, but Whistlers are especially renowned. A "good" rock can be pitched with the exact same effect as a dart, except that a Whistler gains a +1 damage bonus if he hits.

Of course, rocks cause blunt damage (not puncture damage as do darts). Only good rocks that are specially selected by the Whistler gain the above advantage. If just any old rock is being pitched, damage is reduced to 1 (plus any Strength adjustment) and long range becomes 3 (not 4). Good rocks have been worn round in swift rivers. Most rubble, cave rocks, and the broken rocks found in old dungeons are not good rocks. Whistlers usually carry a supply of 2d4 good rocks (thrown rocks that hit their targets can be recovered; those that miss are lost).

Nonweapon Proficiencies: *Bonuses:* Agriculture, Dancing, Spellcraft, Whistling/Humming. *Suggested:* Animal Lore, Astrology, Brewing, Cooking, Crowd Working, Direction Sense, Fire-Building, Fishing, Herbalism, Hunting, Leatherworking, Mountaineering, Musical Instrument, Poetry, Rope Use, Singing, Set Snares, Survival, Swimming, Tracking, Weather Sense.

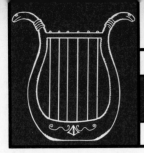

Whistlers generally use fishing, hunting, set snares, and other such skills for the benefit of nature. They learn these skills so they can scare game away from sport hunters, spring snares and traps set by greedy furriers, and so on. Using nature when necessary is acceptable, but it should never be abused. A Whistler will resort to hunting and fishing only if there is no other way to avoid starvation.

Armor/Equipment: Whistlers wear only padded armor. They don't like the thought of wearing leather armor, as some animal had to die for it, and they find other types of armor too restricting and unnatural.

Special Benefits:

Influence Reactions: Although Whistlers use a different form of music, namely whistling and humming, their ability to influence reactions functions exactly like the True Bard's ability of the same name.

Counter Tune: As noted earlier in the demi-human bard section, halfling demi-bards don't cast spells. Rather, they gain a special counter spell ability. Whistlers implement this ability by humming or whistling the proper counter tune. A counter tune must be whistled to counter a spell that has a verbal component; otherwise, the counter tune must be hummed.

Counter tune functions just like counter spell in all other ways.

Chattering: Whistling is a wonderful way to express one's mood, but Whistlers take this form of basic communication a bit further. By "chattering," a process of whistling, trilling, and emitting an occasional squeak, Whistlers are able to communicate. They can carry on complex conversations with other chatterers and are even able to communicate with some animals.

Whistlers can communicate with any naturally occurring animal that can squeak, chirp, or whistle. Such communication is on a fundamental level. Basic information can be exchanged, as well as mood, feelings, *etc.* For example, a Whistler could chatter with a squirrel and learn that it has a lot of nuts hidden in a nearby oak tree. Whistling with a bird might enable the Whistler to learn if it has seen any large monsters (but not if it has seen five ettin or other specific information).

Whistlers often find a forest friend that accompanies them on some of their less dangerous adventures. Ferrets and foxes are particularly fond of adventuring with Whistlers.

Stormwhistle: The phrase "whistle up a storm" was coined when a ranger once witnessed a halfling (actually a Whistler) standing out in the middle of a drought-struck potato field. To the ranger's amazement, the little fellow stuck his hands into his pockets and starting whistling. Puzzled, the ranger crouched behind a large birch and watched. An hour later, the sky had clouded over and it started to rain. After the rain was coming down quite heavily, the ranger glimpsed a satisfied-looking halfling strolling away.

It is true that halflings can't cast wizard spells. However, Whistlers are able to cast certain clerical spells. They do not receive these spells like clerics. In fact, the source of these spells is somewhat of a mystery. Most Whistlers agree that they are granted by Mother Nature herself.

In any event, Whistlers gain the ability to cast each of the following spells once per day. The usual components for these spells are ignored; the Whistler need only whistle to cast the spell. Whistlers gain the following spells at the listed levels:

1st level: *pass without trace*
3rd level: *obscurement*
5th level: *plant growth*
7th level: *speak with plants*
9th level: *control winds*
11th level: *weather summoning*
13th level: *control weather*
15th level: *entangle*

Special Hindrances: As with all halfling demi-bards, Whistlers do not gain the bard ability to cast wizard spells, nor do they gain

the 10th-level bard ability to use any written magical item.

Multi-Classed Bards

As noted in Chapter 3 of the *Player's Handbook* under the discussion of multi-class benefits and restrictions, no multi-classed bards combination were listed. Now that this book is out, it is time to introduce bard multi-class combinations. Note that multi-class options are not open to human characters.

All of the standard demihuman races and their allowable bard multi-classes are listed below. For added flavor, multi-class combinations have been defined for specific kits. If the kits are not used in your campaign, only those combinations that include the True Bard can be used.

Entries such as "Fighter/Chanter * Skald" are a shorthand way of saying "Fighter/Chanter or Fighter/Skald."

Dwarf
Fighter/Chanter * Skald

Elf
Mage/Minstrel
Thief/Gypsy

Gnome
Illusionist/Professor
Thief/Professor * Jongleur

Half-Elf
Fighter/True * Blade * Gallant * Skald
Ranger/True * Meistersinger
Mage/Loremaster * Riddlemaster
Cleric/True
Druid/Meistersinger
Thief/True * Gypsy * Jongleur * Thespian

Halfling
Thief/Jongleur

Dual-Classed Bards

Only humans can be dual-classed. Dual-classed humans can use any kit that the Dungeon Master allows in his campaign.

In order to switch from the bard to another character class, the character must have a 15 or better in both Dexterity and Charisma and a 17 or better in the prime requisite of the new class.

If the character is of another class and wishes to pick up the bard class, he must have a 15 or better in the prime requisite of his other class and a 17 or better in both Dexterity and Charisma.

Following their jack-of-all-trades reputation, bards can learn proficiencies from the general, rogue, warrior, and wizard proficiency groups. Only those proficiencies in the priest group cost an additional slot to gain. However, because most proficiencies fall into more than one group, a lot of proficiencies listed in the priest group are also available to the bard under another group. In fact, of all the proficiencies listed in Chapter 5 of the *Player's Handbook*, only one, healing, is not in one of the bard's proficiency groups. Thus only healing requires the bard to spend an additional slot to acquire (three total).

Compiled Proficiencies

The following table has been compiled in order to assist bard players in selecting their nonweapon proficiencies. **Bold-faced** proficiencies are new proficiencies found only in this book. They are expanded upon later.

Italicized proficiencies require the player to record a specific topic or area that the proficiency covers. For example, the survival proficiency must be specified for a particular environment (e.g., arctic, woodland, desert, steppe, mountain, or tropical). If woodland is chosen, the proficiency is to be recorded as "Survival (Woodland)." Each additional proficiency slot used can either improve the proficiency for a specific topic or it can be used to gain another topic, such as "Survival (Woodland, Steppe)."

New Proficiencies

Acting

Acting enables a character to skillfully portray various roles. Acting is most often used as a form of entertainment; it can also be useful in aiding a disguise. If both acting and disguise are known, the proficiency check for either is made with a +1 bonus.

Proficiency checks are required only if the

actor must portray a particularly difficult character or is attempting an "ad lib" role (*i.e.*, a nonrehearsed role or on short notice).

Chanting

The character is an accomplished chanter and can use this ability to help fellow workers or soldiers keep pace. Proficiency checks are used to determine the effectiveness of the chanting.

On a successful proficiency check, those who can hear the chanter become slightly hypnotized by the rhythmic sound, causing the time spent on arduous, repetitive tasks to pass quickly. The DM can, at his option, adjust results for forced marching, rowing, digging, and other such tasks accordingly.

Table 14: NONWEAPON PROFICIENCIES

Proficiency	Slots Req'd.	Relevant Ability	Mod.
Acting	1	Cha	−1
Agriculture	1	Int	+0
Ancient History	1	Int	−1
Animal Handling	1	Wis	−1
Animal Lore	1	Int	+0
Animal Training	1	Wis	+0
Appraising	1	Int	+0
Armorer	2	Int	−2
Artistic Ability	1	Wis	+0
Astrology	2	Int	+0
Blacksmithing	1	Str	+0
Blind-fighting	2	NA	NA
Bowyer/Fletcher	1	Dex	−1
Brewing	1	Int	+0
Carpentry	1	Str	+0
Chanting	1	Cha	+2
Charioteering	1	Dex	+2
Cobbling	1	Dex	+0
Cooking	1	Int	+0
Craft Instrument	2	Dex	−2
Crowd Working	1	Cha	+0
Dancing	1	Dex	+0

Craft Instrument

Those who take this proficiency must specify whether they are skilled at crafting wind, stringed, percussion, or keyboard instruments. It takes an additional proficiency slot to gain one of the other skills. Three additional slots allow the character to take the title "master craftsman" as he is able to craft instruments of all forms.

A craftsman must buy materials equal to a quarter of the instrument's sale value. It then takes 1d6 days to craft a wind or percussion instrument, 2d8 days to form a stringed instrument, and 3d10 days to create a keyboard instrument. These times assume that the craftsman is spending 10 hours a day working on the instrument. If craftsman tools (cost 25 gp, weight 5 pounds) are not available, all times are doubled.

The quality of an instrument is determined by a final proficiency check. Failure results in an instrument of poor quality, while success indicates good quality. A natural 20 indicates that the instrument is nonfunctional, while a natural 1 results in a masterpiece worth twice the normal value.

Simple repairs take only 1d4 hours and re-

Proficiency	Slots Req'd.	Relevant Ability	Mod.
Direction Sense	1	Wis	+1
Disguise	1	Cha	−1
Endurance	2	Con	+0
Engineering	2	Int	−3
Etiquette	1	Cha	+0
Fire-Building	1	Wis	−1
Fishing	1	Wis	−1
Forgery	1	Dex	−1
Gaming	1	Cha	+0
Gem Cutting	2	Dex	−2
Healing	3*	Wis	−2
Heraldry	1	Int	+0
Herbalism	2	Int	−2
Hunting	1	Wis	−1
Juggling	1	Dex	−1
Jumping	1	Str	+0
Languages, Ancient	1	Int	+0
Languages, Modern	1	Int	+0
Leatherworking	1	Int	+0
Local History	1	Cha	+0
Mining	2	Wis	−3
Mountaineering	1	NA	NA
Musical Instrument	1	Dex	−1
Navigation	1	Int	−2
Poetry	1	Int	−2
Pottery	1	Dex	−2
Reading Lips	2	Int	−2

Proficiency	Slots Req'd.	Relevant Ability	Mod.
Reading/Writing	1	Int	+1
Religion	1	Wis	+0
Riding, Airborne	2	Wis	−2
Riding, Land-based	1	Wis	+3
Rope Use	1	Dex	+0
Running	1	Con	−6
Seamanship	1	Dex	+1
Seamstress/Tailor	1	Dex	−1
Set Snares	1	Dex	−1
Singing	1	Cha	+0
Spellcraft	1	Int	−2
Stonemasonry	1	Str	−2
Survival	2	Int	+0
Swimming	1	Str	+0
Tightrope Walking	1	Dex	+0
Tracking	2	Wis	+0
Tumbling	1	Dex	+0
Ventriloquism	1	Int	−2
Weaponsmithing	3	Int	−3
Weather Sense	1	Wis	−1
Weaving	1	Int	−1
Whistling/Humming	1	Dex	+2

*Healing is not within a bard's proficiency group, thus it takes three slots to learn instead of two as listed in the *Player's Handbook*.

quire no proficiency check unless the proper tools are not available. However, repairing severe damage requires 1d8 hours and a check is mandatory for success.

Crowd Working

Almost every bard is familiar with the ways of a crowd. However, those who take crowd working learn all the tricks of the trade. Such bards are skilled at observing crowds and adjusting their performances accordingly.

Any bard who is using a special ability to adjust the encounter reactions of a crowd (*e.g.*, influence reactions) can make a crowd working proficiency check. If this check is successful, the bard can alter the reactions of the crowd by two levels instead of the typical one.

If the bard or his group is soliciting money from a crowd, a successful proficiency check indicates that the bard is particularly appealing and the crowd willingly donates twice as much money as it normally would (or conditions improve one category if using the performance rules earlier in this handbook).

Poetry

Proficiency in poetry includes the skills of reciting poetry and judging its quality. It also indicates that the character has a repertoire of poems memorized for recital at any time. No proficiency check is required for a normal recital.

If the character can read and write, original poems can be written. A successful proficiency check indicates that the poem is of above average quality.

Whistling/Humming

Almost anyone can whistle or hum. Those who take this proficiency are exceptional whistlers and hummers. They can produce tunes as captivating as most songs. A person with this proficiency is a true master whistler and hummer.

It is so easy to learn a new tune to whistle or hum that characters with this proficiency can learn numerous tunes. In fact, if a proficiency check is made, a whistler or hummer knows any particular tune in question. In addition, a character with both this proficiency and the animal lore proficiency can mimic any bird call he has heard.

However, most adventurers do not take whistling just for the entertainment value. Instead, they are looking for its uses in communication. This communication is possible only among those who know this proficiency. If both characters succeed with their proficiency checks, a single concept can be communicated. Some examples are "Go around to the side door," "I hear them coming," "Slowly reach out now, the guard doesn't see you."

This section examines most of the core bard's common abilities. These include pick pockets, detect noise, climb walls, read languages, and the bard's 10th-level ability to use any written magical item.

The first four of these abilities are collectively known as a bard's "thief skills," as they mimic the thief skills of the same name. As stated in the *Player's Handbook* under the section on the thief class, thief skills cannot be raised above 95%, no matter what modifiers are applied.

Pick Pockets

The ability to pick pockets extends far beyond reaching into a victim's coat pocket and removing its contents. It has many other applications, as listed below. Some of these applications can be reversed and are indicated below. For example, "Redo" is the opposite of "Undo."

- Undo/Redo: A bard can untie, unstring, unclasp, unbuckle, unbutton, *etc.*, an item without being noticed.
- Palm/Place: Palming enables a bard's hand to be held naturally while looking empty, but it actually contains some item: cards, a dagger, a scroll, silverware, coins (up to 10 + 2/level), gems (up to 5 + 1/level), *etc.*
- Lift/Drop: Lifting is the art of removing small items from others' pockets, sleeves, girdles, packs, *etc.*, without the victims noticing.
- Strip/Garb: If a bard removes any accessible item (small or large) from a sleeping person (swords, boots, hat, and so on) without waking the victim, he is stripping items from the victim.
- Sleight of Hand: This is a general category that enables a bard to transfer an item from one hand to another, make the item seem alive, make it vanish and reappear, cause it to appear behind another's ear, and so on.
- Adjust Items: This skill enables a bard to make subtle adjustments without being noticed. For example, a bard could slip a peg

from hole 1 of some game into hole 2.
- Exchange: Exchange enables a bard to reach into a pile of coins and remove more than he places there or to drop in a gold but remove a platinum.
- Slit: Slitting is the art of cutting through straps or cutting holes in bags, garments, purses, pouches, *etc.*, without being noticed.

Most of these pick pockets functions can be reversed. So doing requires a successful pick pockets roll. An example follows.

While enjoying a fancy dinner party, the bard, Rembam, may wish to frame the good cleric Baldwin as a thief. To do so he might undo Madam Morgava's necklace, lift it from her, then drop it in Baldwin's pocket (this process requires three pick pockets rolls).

Later Rembam could alter the topic of discussion to that of jewelry, causing Madam Morgava to notice her missing necklace. As soon as a large stir is made, Rembam might exclaim, "I noticed the good cleric here was doting over your person earlier. Perhaps we should ask him to empty his pockets."

Success/Failure/Detection: If a bard rolls equal to or below his pick pockets score, he succeeds in the attempt. If he rolls above his pick pockets score, he fails. However, success and failure are separate from being detected. A bard's attempt to lift a gem from a merchant's pocket might be detected regardless of whether the bard succeeds in his attempt.

Detection is determined by subtracting three times the victim's (or observer's) level from 100. If the bard's roll is equal to or above this number, his attempt is detected (regardless of the attempt's success or failure).

Detect Noise

Bards are attentive to every sound or noise, no matter how small or seemingly insignificant, including faint sounds that most others miss.

The rules listed in the *Player's Handbook* under the thief and bard classes (as well as in the *Dungeon Master's Guide* under "Listening" in Chapter 15) state that a listener may attempt to pick up faint sounds any time he wants, simply by standing still and listening for one round. Any head gear (hat, helmet, *etc.*) must be removed and there cannot be any noise in the immediate vicinity (*i.e.*, party members must be quiet). The check is made secretly by the Dungeon Master. Success means that the listener picks up some noise. Additional checks can be made in which the listener can attempt to discern one of the following (per check):

• number of beings
• race
• nature of beings
• exact direction
• movement
• bits of conversation
• distance to beings

Once a check fails, no more information can be gained unless conditions change considerably (and favorably).

If you would like to add greater detail to your character's chance to hear noise, consider using Table 15.

Climb Walls

There is an entire section in the *Player's Handbook* devoted to this skill. It is found in Chapter 14: Time and Movement. It is important to note that bards perform just like thieves when it comes to climbing walls. Any climbing walls comment that applies to thieves also applies to bards. For example, in the *Player's Handbook*, thieves are given a number of special climbing benefits, which all apply to bards as well.

Although most adventurers can climb rocky cliffs and steep slopes, rogues (including bards) are far superior to others in this ability. They not only succeed more often

Table 15: DETECT NOISE MODIFIERS
(Optional)

Situation	Modifier
*Distance (indoor/outdoor)**	
Up to 5 feet/yards	+10%
Up to 25 feet/yards	—
Up to 50 feet/yards	−10%
Up to 100 feet/yards	−25%
Up to 150 feet/yards	−50%
Up to 200 feet/yards	−75%
Up to 300 feet/yards	−100%
Ear Covering	
Cap	−10%
Scarf/Cloth	−10%
Hat	−25%
Leather helmet	−50%
Metal helmet	−75%
Sound Obstructions	
Closed door	−50%
Ear pressed to door	−20%
Bend in corridor	−10%
Curtains	−15%
Sound Volume	
Whisper	−25%
Personal conversation	—
Speaking to an audience	+10%
Shouting	+25%
Yelling	+50%

*Distances are measured in feet indoors and in yards outdoors.

than others, but they can climb even the most difficult surfaces without the aid of special gear (called free climbing). Rogues are the only characters who can climb rough, smooth, and very smooth surfaces without the use of ropes or other equipment. And they are the only characters able to climb very smooth surfaces when they are slightly slippery.

For your convenience, all climb walls rules that apply to bards have been compiled and are listed here in an easy-to-use format.

Mountaineering Proficiency: Every proficiency slot spent on mountaineering (including the initial slot) increases a bard's climb walls score by 10%. The bard is not required to use climbing gear in order to gain this benefit. It is a permanent increase that applies in all situations.

Table 16: CLIMBING MODIFIERS

Situation	Modifier
Miscellaneous	
Rope and wall*	+55%
Encumbrance**	−5%
Climber below half hp	−10%
Rappelling down a surface	
Bottom of rope is held	+50%
Bottom of rope is not held	+30%
Surface condition	
Abundant handholds (brush, trees, ledges)	+40%
Sloped inward	+25%
Slightly slippery (wet or crumbling)	−25%
Slippery (icy, slimy)	−40%

*Assisted Climbs (Using Climbing Tools)****

Armor Type	Assisted Bonus	Total Modifier
No Armor****	—	+10%
Leather Armor	—	—
Padded Armor	+25%	−5%
Studded Leather	+25%	−5%
Ring Mail	+10%	−15%
Brigandine	—	−25%
Scale Mail	+30%	−15%
Hide Armor	+25%	−5%
Chain Mail	+10%	−15%
Elven Chain	+15%	−5%
Splint Mail	—	−25%
Banded Armor	+65%	−25%
Plate Mail	+45%	−50%
Bronze Plate	+45%	−50%
Field Plate	+45%	−50%
Full Plate	+45%	−50%

*This bonus applies when the character can brace his feet against the wall and use the rope to assist in the climb.

**This penalty is cumulative for each encumbrance category worse than unencumbered (*e.g.*, a moderately encumbered bard would suffer a −10% penalty).

***The armor adjustments to a bard's climb walls percentage, given on Tables 9 and 10 in the "Creation" section, apply to bards performing free climbs (*i.e.*, climbs in which pitons, rope, and so on aren't used, which is the norm for rogues). When a bard uses climbing tools, he is performing an assisted climb. Assisted climbers suffer less severe armor penalties, as ropes can be coiled about and attached to their armor, and they are able to lean out from the wall more, making the bulkiness of their armor less significant.

The "Assisted Bonus" column can be used by players who want to record only their free climbing percentage (*i.e.*, their climbing walls score has been adjusted as per Table 9 or 10 in the "Creation" section). The "Total Modifier" column lists the result of combining the armor penalty with the assisted climb bonus.

As an example, studded leather normally causes a −30% climbing penalty. If tools are used, a bonus of 25% is added, making the penalty for assisted climbing in studded leather only −5%.

****Includes small magical items such as rings, bracers, cloaks, but no large or bulky devices.

Climbing Checks: A climbing check must be made any time a bard tries to climb more than 10 feet. According to the *Player's Handbook* (Chapter 14: Time and Movement), an initial check is made to see if the bard is able to even attempt the climb. If this check fails, the wall is too difficult and another attempt can be made only if the bard's chance to succeed increases (*i.e.*, a

rope is tossed down) or he moves to a significantly different new location (half a mile or more along a cliff).

Another check is not required unless the bard climbs more than 100 feet or takes more than a turn (ten rounds) to climb. The reason for this is that the first check assumes that the bard is scouting out the wall (or cliff), picking the best route. If the check is successful, he has found such a route and can climb the surface safely.

Optional Rule: It should take one turn to scout out a surface. If the surface cannot be seen or scouted for some reason, the bard must simply start climbing and hope for the best. In such cases, a climb walls check is made; if it fails, the bard falls. To determine how high he had climbed, roll a percentile die and that is the fraction of the climb that had been completed before the fall.

For example, if Aldwin is adventuring in a large underground cavern and decides to climb a wall, he spends a turn examining what he can see (say 15 feet in torch light). He then rolls his climb walls check. If successful, he sees an obvious route and can climb up to 15 feet without mishap. If he decides to climb the other 50 feet of this 65-foot-high wall, he must roll a second check (it is impossible to scout in the middle of a climb). He rolls and fails; now the DM rolls a percentile of 98. Aldwin almost reaches the top before he falls. The DM decides that the damage should be 6d6 as Aldwin essentially falls 60 feet.

Falling: As always, falling damage is 1d6 per 10 feet. A fall of 40 feet causes 4d6 damage.

If a climber is climbing assisted (using tools), he cannot fall clear to the ground. If pitons or spikes are being driven into a wall and rope is attached between them and a climber, the climber will fall only until the slack between him and the piton is taken up.

Thus, if the climber attaches 20 feet of rope to the piton, climbs 10 feet up, and then falls,

he would fall 30 feet (10 feet down to the piton plus the 20 feet of slack) and suffer 3d6 points of damage (the DM might decide to allow a saving throw vs. paralyzation for half damage, since the rope takes up some of the shock).

Pitons and spikes are not completely reliable and pull out 15% of the time.

Characters can also rope themselves together. If a roped character falls, any character directly tied to him must immediately roll a climbing check. Success stops the fall, failure means that they are both falling. If more than one person is falling, a −10% penalty results for every falling character in addition to the first one (*e.g.*, if three characters are falling the penalty would be −20%).

Climbing Rates: To determine how fast a bard climbs, look for the type of surface and the surface condition on the following table. Multiply the resulting number by the character's current movement rate. That is the number of feet per round the bard can travel in any direction (up, down, sideways, or diagonal). This rate is twice as fast as nonrogues can travel.

Table 17: BARD CLIMBING RATES

Type of Surface	Dry	Slightly Slippery	Slippery
Very smooth	1/2	1/4	—
Smooth, cracked	1	2/3	1/2
Rough	2	2/3	1/2
Rough w/ledges	2	1	2/3
Ice wall	—	—	1/2
Tree	8	6	4
Sloping wall	6	4	2
Rope and wall	4	2	1
Rappelling	10	10	10

Combat While Climbing: Combat is both difficult and dangerous while climbing. Spells can be cast only if the bard is in a steady, braced position. If the spell has a material

component, the bard must have one hand free. Somatic components require the use of both hands (*i.e.*, the bard must be able to steady himself with rope and legs alone).

The following additional adjustments occur while climbing:

- Dexterity and shield Armor Class bonuses are lost.
- Most attacks against a climber are made with the +2 rear attack bonus.
- Climbers suffer a −2 penalty to attack, damage, and saving rolls.
- Attacking from above results in a +2 attack roll bonus and attacking from below results in a −2 attack roll penalty. These two adjustments apply to climbers and nonclimbers alike.
- Two-handed weapons are rarely usable by climbers.
- If struck for any amount of damage while climbing, an immediate climbing check must be rolled. A free-climbing character falls if this roll fails, while an assisted climber loses his balance for a round (he can't attack, suffers an additional −2 penalty to saving throws, and opponents gain an additional +2 bonus to their attack rolls).

All adjustments are cumulative. Thus, an ogre standing atop a cliff gains a +6 to attack if Aldwin has lost his balance on his assisted climb (+2 because Aldwin is below the ogre, +2 because Aldwin's back is exposed as he is facing the cliff, and +2 because he is off balance).

Reading, Writing, and Speaking

This section clarifies the differences and similarities between the multiple ways in which a bard can attempt to read, write, and speak languages. In particular the following will be examined: the thief ability read languages; the proficiencies of reading/writing, ancient languages, and modern languages; the

spell *read magic*; and the 10th-level bard ability to use any written magical item. Each has its own specific functions, but the various uses overlap.

The thief ability to read languages enables any rogue, including the bard subclass, to attempt to read any material (other languages, maps, ideograms, *etc.*) that the character isn't proficient in reading. This skill does not enable a thief to read writings that others can read only by using a *read magic* spell (*i.e.*, magical writings cannot be read with the read languages ability). The thief's ability to read languages does not impart the ability to write or speak a language.

All three of the language-oriented proficiencies require the player to record a specific language when the proficiency is first learned. Additional proficiency slots can be spent to gain additional languages, which must also be specified and recorded. Characters automatically succeed when using these three proficiencies (*i.e.*, no proficiency check is rolled) under most circumstances. Only when the proficiency is used in extreme cases, such as reading a very old document or speaking odd dialects, is a proficiency check rolled.

The proficiency reading/writing enables a character to both read and write a specific language—no proficiency check is rolled and there is no need to roll against read languages. Only a "modern" language can be selected as the topic of this proficiency, and only if the character already knows how to speak the language. (A modern language is any language that is currently being used in the character's known campaign world. If a language is not modern, it is always "ancient.")

The modern languages proficiency enables a character to speak a specific language, but not read or write it.

Ancient languages is a unique proficiency that combines the functions of the above two proficiencies with respect to ancient languages. When an ancient language is specified for this proficiency, the player must decide whether the character is fluent in the language (knows how to speak it) or if the character is literate in the language (can read and write it)—both are not immediately gained. If both skills are desired, an additional proficiency slot must be spent on the same language.

The spell *read magic* enables a caster to read, but not write or speak, any writing that is magical. It doesn't matter what language it is written in or who wrote it, only that it is magical. Once read, the caster can read it at any later time without the use of the spell. If the writing isn't magical, this spell has absolutely no effect.

The bard's 10th-level ability to use any written magical item (with a 15% chance of using it incorrectly) is a very special case. By the 10th level, bards have finally learned enough magical symbols and signs that they are able to puzzle through them without the use of *read magic*, *read languages*, or any other aid.

However, a bard does not exactly understand the effects of an item until he first uses it. Up until that time, he has only a vague idea as to the item's general use (*e.g.*, the bard might know that a *flame strike* scroll contains an offensive fire spell). He must read the scroll and activate its magic to learn the exact nature of the scroll.

Note that at 10th level the bard can ignore class restrictions for all magical items of a written nature.

Spell Books

Unlike wizards, bards do not engage in the systematic study of magic or the pursuit of specific spells. In spite of this, most bards pick up some magical knowledge in the course of their travels. However, understanding the meaning of a spell is a difficult task. Spell books are not filled with lines of neatly written text. Instead, they contain arcane formulae, strange symbols, notes, comments, odd runes, *etc.* Understanding them is difficult, as spells aren't "read" like normal writing; they are "solved" like complex mathematical equations, and impressed upon the mind by an act of will.

Only those able to cast spells can attempt to unlock their secrets and tap the energies needed to cast them. The only way to do this is for the spellcaster to successfully roll under his "chance to learn spells" score, which is a function of Intelligence. Once understood, no further attempts to solve a given spell need to be made as long as the spell book is available for study. Note that a spellcaster cannot understand a spell of a level higher than he can currently cast.

Musical Components

Most bards are almost magically skilled at some form of musical expression. If you are seeking a way to more closely incorporate this talent with a bard's magical abilities, you may want to consider the option of using music as the verbal component to spells. Then, instead of speaking arcane words to invoke a spell, the bard sings a song, recites poetry, or plays a tune.

Of course, as with all optional rules, you must first obtain your Dungeon Master's approval. If this option is taken, a bard can perform some form of music in place of a spell's verbal component. However, once this option is agreed upon for your bard, he can no longer speak words to cast spells requiring verbal components. He must always resort to music. Only one of the three musical mediums (singing, poetry, or instrumental) works for any particular bard (until 10th level). Demi-bards have different options available to them. The musical options for bards and demi-bards are given in Table 18.

Table 18:
VERBAL COMPONENT SUBSTITUTES

Kit	Musical Substitute
True	Singing or Instrumental*
Blade	Poetry
Charlatan	Singing
Gallant	Poetry
Gypsy	Instrumental
Herald	Instrumental
Jester	Poetry, Singing, or Instrumental*
Jongleur	Poetry
Loremaster	Instrumental
Meistersinger	Instrumental
Riddlemaster	Poetry
Skald	Singing
Thespian	Singing
Demi-Bards	
Chanter	Chanting
Minstrel	Special**
Professor	Whistling or Instrumental*
Whistler	Whistling

*The bard must select only one of these options. This choice is binding and cannot be altered at a later time.

**Minstrels are a special case. Refer to their kit description.

New Spells

Alter Instrument

(Alteration)

Level: 1
Range: Touch
Components: V, S
Duration: 1 turn/level
Casting Time: 1
Area of Effect: 1 instrument
Saving Throw: None

By using this spell, the caster can transform one musical instrument into another of similar size and equal value. Any hand-held instrument can be altered into any other hand-held instrument. However, in order to obtain a large instrument, such as a base harp, organ, or any other instrument that is too large or heavy to be easily carried, the spellcaster must start with an equally large instrument.

In any event, the value of the new instrument is identical to the original. A golden recorder will generate a silver plated lute, a child's drum will generate a nonfunctional lyre, *etc.*

Bards use this spell to save both money and equipment carried. It is a lot cheaper to buy a single instrument and alter it when another is needed than to buy every instrument that might be required. This also saves a lot of space in one's backpack.

If the instrument the bard wishes to alter is being carried or played by another character, a successful attack roll against the opponent's Armor Class must be made in order to touch the instrument.

Sound Bubble

(Abjuration, Evocation)

Level: 1
Range: 0
Components: V, S, M
Duration: 10 rounds + 1 round/level
Casting Time: 1
Area of Effect: Special
Saving Throw: None

When this spell is cast, an invisible bubble springs into existence. It can either be centered on and mobile with the caster or cast on an area. The mobile bubble has a radius of 10 feet, while the area bubble has a radius of 5 feet per caster level. The bubble has only one effect: sound can't pass through it. Thus sound generated within the bubble can't be heard by those on the outside and vice versa.

Bards often use this spell to enhance the quality and effect of their performances. It also functions nicely when a bard wishes to use one of his talents in a dungeon or other limited setting in which noise is sure to draw unwanted attention.

Besides its entertainment functions, *sound bubble* is also useful in many of the same situations in which *silence* is used.

The material component of the spell is a blown egg shell or a soap bubble.

Silence 15' Radius

(Alteration)

Level: 2
Range: 60 yards
Components: V, S
Duration: 2 rounds/level
Casting Time: 5
Area of Effect: 15-foot-radius sphere
Saving Throw: None

Upon casting this spell, complete silence prevails in the affected area. All sound is stopped: conversation is impossible, spells with verbal components cannot be cast, and no noise issues from or enters the area. The spell can be cast into the air or upon an object, but the effect is stationary unless cast on a mo-

bile object or creature. The spell lasts two rounds for each level of the experience of the caster. If the spell is centered on a creature, the effect then radiates from the creature and moves as it moves. An unwilling creature receives a saving throw vs. spell. If successful, the spell effect is centered about one foot behind the position of the creature at the instant of casting (the effect does not move with the creature in this case). This spell provides a defense against sound-based attacks, such as harpy singing, a *horn of blasting*, etc.

Improved Magic Mouth

(Alteration)

Level: 3
Range: 10 yards
Components: V, S, M
Duration: Special
Casting Time: 3
Area of Effect: 1 object
Saving Throw: None

This spell works in all ways like the 2nd-level wizard spell *magic mouth*, except as follows.

When this spell is cast, the mouth is endowed with the bard's current knowledge, Intelligence, and personality. When the predetermined event occurs that activates the mouth, it converses as if the bard were actually there. For example, the mouth might say, "Who goes there?" and wait for a reply. If the visitors announce their names, it could go on to say, "Tarnak, please proceed to the music room, while the rest wait in the sitting room."

The mouth lasts until the conversation is over.

Although the mouth can be set to activate due to a visual stimulus (*i.e.*, activate if anyone wearing a green feather approaches the castle gate), once triggered, it reacts only to sounds and speech. Also note that the mouth and the bard are not linked in any way. Once

cast, the mouth's knowledge is set and will never change. Thus, if a bard is extremely angry at Tarnak when he casts an *improved magic mouth*, the mouth will remain in a state of anger, even if the bard and Tarnak have reconciled.

Instant Audience

(Conjuration)

Level: 3
Range: 30 yards
Components: V, S, M
Duration: Up to 4 hours
Casting Time: 2
Area of Effect: 1 room or area within range
Saving Throw: None

When this spell is cast, audience members are magically conjured. Each round 1d4 people enter the room or area in a normal manner. (They actually appear just outside the room when no one is looking.) This continues for a number of rounds equal to the caster's level.

The audience contains a combination of races, gender, and social class appropriate to the occasion.

Instant audience members act in every way like any other members of the audience. They walk around during intermission, talk, eat snacks, and so on. However, they always evade questions about their past, their history, or current events, as they have no past, no history, and have no idea as to what is going on in the world outside of the room.

Instant audience members are strictly non-combative and never attack or cast spells (although they can be bullies or braggarts if that is appropriate). If one suffers even a single point of damage, he instantly vanishes along with all of his items (including items no longer on his body, such as clothes that he hung in the linen closet).

Once the performance ends, instant audi-

ence members leave in an appropriate manner and vanish as soon as they are out of view.

If the audience is treated in an inappropriate way (as determined by the DM), the spell instantly ends. For example, an audience could be summoned to watch a combat, but if the audience is used as a human shield, it vanishes.

The material components are a small collection of the items carried by the appropriate audience (a gold coin, a piece of fine fabric, a snuff box, etc.). These are tossed into a bag that contains at least one live mouse. The mouse is not destroyed, but vanishes during the spell to reappear somewhere in the room after the spell ends.

Wall of Sound

(Evocation)

Level: 3
Range: 60 yards
Components: V, S, M
Duration: Concentration + 1 round/level
Casting Time: 3
Area of Effect: Special
Saving Throw: None

The *wall of sound* spell brings forth an immobile, shimmering curtain of violently disturbed air. The wall is made up of a number of 10'x10' sections equal to the caster's level. These sections can be arranged as desired as long as the resulting wall all lies in one plane (*i.e.*, it must be flat) that stands up vertically.

One side of the wall, selected by the caster, produces a voluminous roar that completely disrupts all communication, command words, verbal spell components, and any other form of organized sound within 30 feet. In addition, those within 10 feet are deafened for 1d4 turns if they fail a saving throw vs. spell.

On the other side of the wall, a loud roar can be heard, but communication is possible by shouting, and verbal components and

command words function normally.

Anyone passing through the wall suffers 1d8 points of damage and is permanently deafened unless he rolls a successful saving throw vs. spell. Deafened creatures suffer a −1 penalty to surprise rolls, a +1 penalty to their initiative rolls, and they are 20% likely to miscast spells with a verbal component.

A *silence 15' radius* spell cast by a higher level caster specifically for this purpose will dispel the wall; the wall otherwise destroys all *silence* spells that come into contact with it.

The material component is a piece of slate and a finger nail clipping.

Conjure Cabinet

(Conjuration)

Level: 4
Range: 10 feet
Components: V, S
Duration: 1 round/level
Casting Time: 4
Area of Effect: Special
Saving Throw: None

This is a very special spell created specifically for the bard class. Before this spell can be used, the bard must have a special cabinet made. It must be of the highest quality, worth at least 1,000 gold pieces. It can be any size up to 4 feet wide by 4 feet deep by 8 feet high.

Once the cabinet is made, this spell must be cast upon it and the cabinet must be named. At any later date, the bard can cast this spell and the cabinet temporarily teleports to the bard's current location. The cabinet carries with it any contents that are of a performing nature usable by the bard. (For example, it might contain musical instruments, cleaning tools, a playing stool, etc., for a True Bard. It might be lined with throwing daggers, rapiers [for sword swallowing], and blindfolds for a Blade).

When the cabinet teleports to the bard, a

percentile die must be rolled. On a 01-04, it appears 2d20 feet in the air and falls, destroying itself (but its contents are recoverable). On a roll of 99-00, it teleports into the ground and is destroyed. Otherwise, it is safe.

The cabinet remains for the duration of the spell or until the bard speaks the cabinet's name. It then teleports safely back to its previous location, along with any carried items of a performing nature usable by the bard.

A bard may have only one such cabinet at a time. The teleport will not carry the cabinet to another plane. If items of a nonperforming nature are left in the cabinet, then the cabinet will not teleport.

Magical Items

As is the nature of bards, they meddle in everything, including magical items created by the great wizards of past and present. Below you will find a list of new magical items, old magical items, and new ways to use old magical items.

New Magical Items

Case of Compression: When empty, this musical instrument case appears as any other such case. However, when touched to any instrument normally carried in a case, it transforms so that it perfectly fits the instrument. When the case is closed with the instrument inside, it shrinks until it easily fits in the palm of the hand. The reduced case weighs only a pound. When the case is opened, it returns itself and its instrument to full size.

About 10% of these cases are cursed; such cases devour the instrument 25% of the time.

Gourd of Travel: By shaking this gourd and saying the command word, the bard is able to teleport himself and one other to any known place. A *gourd of travel* does not allow for travel between planes.

A *gourd of travel* has 1d10 seeds within it, which produce the rattling sound that causes the gourd to function. Every time the gourd is used, one of these seeds vanishes. When the last seed vanishes, the gourd becomes a nonmagical item.

Harp of Healing: When this magical harp is played within 10 feet of wounded creatures, it heals each creature by one point per hour of playing. However, once the music stops or a new player takes over, further playing is useless unless new wounds are received.

After eight hours of continuous playing, a bard must begin to make successful Constitution rolls once an hour or he misplays the harp and healing ends.

Horn of Amplification: This horn is not hollow as one would expect. Rather, it is solid and resembles the horn of a rhinoceros. It is used by touching its base to the forehead. It magically attaches and conveys its special power. At this time, the one wearing the horn has his voice amplified from two to ten times in volume. The exact increase is up to the character using the horn. The horn has no other function. It can be removed by anyone who lightly pulls on it.

This horn increases the range of all songs, jokes, rhymes, and other forms of verbal communication proportionately (*e.g.*, an amplification of five increases the range by five times the normal distance).

The character can also yell. A yell causes 2d10 points of damage to everyone except the user within a range of 5 feet times the amplification (*e.g.*, setting 2 has a 10-foot range, setting 5 has a 25-foot range, *etc.*). A successful saving throw vs. petrification reduces damage by half. Only one yell per encounter can be attempted.

Each time the horn is used, there is a 1% chance that it permanently affixes to the user's forehead and loses all magical ability. It can then be used as a weapon for head butts, causing 1d3 points of damage. However, the oddity of having a horn growing from the character's head results in a −2 Charisma penalty. A *wish* must be used to remove the horn.

Horn of Baubles: When this instrument is blown, one 5'x5'x5' cube of useless baubles spews out of it per level of the blower. Although this is usually rather comical, it can be dangerous in a limited space.

The instrument can be safely blown once every hour. If blown more frequently, there is a 10% cumulative chance that the horn backfires, sucking the blower into it and spewing him out as a collection of useless baubles. It is impossible to resurrect or reincarnate a creature in this state, although a *wish* can be used to recover the victim.

Lyre of Wounding: This cursed item appears normal in every way until it is first played. When the musician's fingers strike its strings, they sever the tips of his fingers. Roll 1d6 for the number of fingers that the musician loses: 1-4 = the number of lost fingers, 5 = all fingers and the thumb, and 6 = escaped unscathed. Each finger lost causes 1d2 points of damage, but the musician should not be lowered below 1 hit point due to lost fingers.

Each lost finger causes the musician's proficiency at playing musical instruments to suffer a penalty of −2. Other proficiencies and activities requiring manual dexterity are likewise reduced, at the DM's discretion. Lost digits can be regenerated magically.

As with cursed swords, whenever the musician decides to play, the lyre leaps into his hands; magically altering the form of the instrument does not abate its curse.

Periapt of Proof Against Sound: This small periapt is indistinguishable from other gems. The character who has this periapt gains extra resistance to any sound-based attack or influence. If a saving throw is normally allowed, the periapt provides an extra bonus to the saving throw. The level of the bonus depends upon the quality of the periapt, as follows:

D100	Save Bonus
01-40	+1
41-60	+2
61-75	+3
76-90	+4
91-95	+5
96-00	+1, 5' radius

If no saving throw is usually allowed, the periapt provides a normal saving throw vs. spell against the sound. A *periapt of proof against sound* affects all hostile sounds, including harpy singing, sirens, screams or shrieks that cause damage or fear, all musical influences (including bard abilities), spells that rely upon verbal communication to affect their victims (*e.g., command, suggestion, etc.*), and so on. However, the periapt has no effect upon communication, such as, "Kill that stupid bard!," verbal components for spells, magical item command words, or any other sound that does not directly affect the individual who has the periapt.

Pick of Strumming: This magical pick enables the user to play any stringed instrument that is normally plucked with fingers or a pick. This includes harps, lutes, mandolins, *etc.* The person grasping the pick can play any song he has ever heard. The pick's magic is so great that all functions of the instrument are instantly mastered. Thus, the bard automatically knows the proper grips to use on the lute, how to hold the harp, how to adjust the strings of the mandolin, *etc.* His skill level rivals that of a master musician proficient in the instrument's use.

Also, a bard who uses this pick to play the *lyre of wounding* does not suffer any severed fingers.

Recorder of Recording: This recorder has two magical functions. If, after a song is played on it, the bard says, "Play it again when X happens," the recorder will magically play the entire song over again any time condition X occurs (*e.g.,* "When Tarnak comes within 20 feet.").

The other magical function is activated by speaking the word, "record," before playing a song. At any later time, the bard can say, "play back," and the recorder produces all sounds that it recorded within 30 feet during the song. Furthermore, these sounds are played back as if the recorder hadn't been making any noise at the time.

The recorder does not reproduce special sound-based attacks of any sort.

Zither of Speed: This zither appears to be a normal musical instrument. However, if it is played in a rapid tempo and the musician says, "Adagietto," all allies within 30 feet are affected as if under the influence of a *haste* spell.

If the zither is played slowly and "Adagissimo" is spoken, all foes within 30 feet are affected as if under a *slow* spell (no saving throw). The effects last as long as the bard concentrates upon the music or until he plays the zither at a moderate tempo and says, "Andante." If he moves, defends himself, suffers damage, rolls for a saving throw, or performs any other action, his concentration is broken.

A *zither of speed* functions only once per day. Furthermore, for every successive day in a row that its magic is used, there is a 10% cumulative chance that one of its strings breaks, rendering the item useless unless it can be repaired.

Old Magical Items

The following magical items are all located in the *Dungeon Master's Guide*; they are particularly suited to or favored by bards. *Italicized* entries are cursed or are items that bards find particularly distasteful.

Potions
Philter of Glibness
Philter of Stammering and Stuttering
Ventriloquism
Rods
Beguiling
Rulership
Splendor

Miscellaneous Magic (Noninstrumental)
Boots of Dancing
Helm of Comprehending Languages and
    Reading Magic
Sheet of Smallness
Tome of Leadership and Influence

Miscellaneous Magic (Musical Instruments)
Chime of Hunger
Chime of Interruption
Chime of Opening
Drums of Deafening
Drums of Panic
Harp of Charming
Harp of Discord
Horn of Blasting
Horn of Bubbles
Horn of Collapsing
Horn of Fog
Horn of Goodness (Evil)
Horn of Valhalla
Lyre of Building
Pipes of Haunting
Pipes of Pain
Pipes of Sounding
Pipes of the Sewers

Weapons and Armor
Armor of Command
Elven Chain Mail
Sword of Dancing

New Twists on Old Items

(Optional Rules)

This optional section contains suggested special effects that occur when various bard kits use the instruments and other magical

items listed above. All of these suggestions are optional, but will make for a lot of added flavor and fun in your campaign.

Because bards are so musically inclined, their understanding of all musical instruments, including magical items, is such that they gain certain special benefits. This is also true of several other magical items that are specially related to bards.

Elven Minstrels: Because these special demi-bards understand the union of magic and music better than anyone, they gain a special benefit. Any time a hazardous magical effect based on music occurs, an elven Minstrel gains a +2 bonus to the saving throw. Success indicates that the hazardous effect is avoided. If no saving throw is allowed, this allows one at the normal chance for success.

Philter of Glibness: If a Charlatan imbibes this potion, even *detect lie* will have only a 5% chance to note any "stretching of the truth."

Philter of Stammering and Stuttering: This potion functions as a *philter of glibness* or *persuasiveness* when imbibed by a Jester and has no ill effects.

Boots of Dancing: These boots have no effect upon a Jester.

Helm of Comprehending Languages and Reading Magic: When worn by a bard, this helm grants the ability to understand 95% of strange writings and 90% of magical writings. If the bard is 10th level or higher, the chance to understand magical writings rises to 95%.

Tome of Leadership and Influence: When this is read by a bard, the character increases by one level. His experience points become equal to the minimum required to attain the new level.

Unless stated otherwise, the following notes apply only to bard kits that have Musical Instrument listed as a bonus proficiency. Those kits that have Musical Instrument listed as a suggested proficiency are also affected, but

only if the bard in question is proficient with the particular instrument.

Chime of Hunger: When struck by a bard, this chime's cursed powers radiate out 60 feet + 10 feet per level of the bard.

Chime of Interruption: When this is used by a bard, affected spellcasters must roll their saving throws with a −1 penalty per three levels of the bard. Elven Minstrels disrupt any spell that they can themselves cast.

Chime of Opening: Bards can attempt to destroy locks, lids, doors, valves, and portals with this chime (in addition to its normal functions). The chance to destroy is equal to 5% per level of the bard. Thus a 6th-level bard would have a 30% chance to destroy such an item. The maximum chance is 95%. Of course, if the bard doesn't want to destroy the item, he can use the chime normally.

Drums of Deafening: These drums are a pair of kettle drums, but bards can invoke the magic in each drum separately. If the left drum is struck, it causes those within 10 feet to be stunned for 2d4 rounds. If the right drum is struck, it causes all within 70 feet to be permanently deafened (a *heal* spell or similar magic is needed to regain hearing). Dwarven Chanters can double all areas of effect.

Drums of Panic: If these drums are struck by a bard, the radius of the inner "safe zone" can be reduced to any desired measurement. Affected creatures suffer a saving throw penalty of −1 penalty per three levels of the bard.

Harp of Charming: Once per turn a bard is able to cause the harp to cast a *command* spell as a caster equal to the bard's level.

Harp of Discord: Unfortunately for bards, their greater musical talents cause the effects of this instrument to last for 2d4 +2 rounds after the music stops. Jesters cause the effect to last for 2d4 turns.

Horn of Blasting: Bards are better able to play this instrument, so that there is only a 5% cumulative chance per day that the horn will explode. Furthermore, the listed "2% cumulative chance of the instrument self-de-

structing" is reduced to 1%.

Horn of Bubbles: Bards are actually able to use this cursed magical item to their advantage (once they determine what the horn is). When properly blown by a bard, the horn emits a cone of bubbles 30 feet long with a 30-foot diameter end. Anyone caught in the bubbles is effectively blinded for 2d10 rounds unless he rolls a successful saving throw vs. breath weapon. However, there is a 5% chance that the horn backfires and sucks the bard through it, emitting him as a mass of bubbles. Once all of the bubbles pop (taking 2d10 rounds), the bard is irrevocably dead. Jesters have only a 1% chance of being turned to bubbles.

Horn of Collapsing: Bards have only a 5% chance of sounding the horn improperly. Dwarven Chanters never use this instrument improperly once they know the command word.

Horn of Fog: When this horn is blown, bards are able to create the typical fog, or they can create a region of magical rain. Rain can be very useful as a source of water, to put out fires, or to fill the bottom of a room with water. The rain will accumulate 1 inch of water per round in a 10-foot square.

Horn of Goodness (Evil): Unfortunately for many bards, sounding this instrument might produce an alignment change. There is a 50% chance that the bard becomes neutral evil, otherwise he becomes neutral good. If the bard is already one of these two alignments, the horn functions normally.

Horn of the Tritons: Bards are able to sound this horn even though it isn't normally usable by rogues. Meistersingers and halfling Whistlers are able to use this magical horn twice per day.

Horn of Valhalla: At 5th level bards can sound the brass horn, at 10th level the bronze horn, and at 15th level the iron horn. Skalds can play any of these horns without penalty.

Lyre of Building: A bard can negate the effects of a *horn of blasting*, a *disintegrate* spell, or the effect of up to three rounds of attack

from a ram or similar siege item. This works once per day for every three levels of the bard. When the lyre is used to perform work, a bard is able to achieve the work of 100 men + 10 men per level of the bard. If a bard should happen to fail the false chord check, a saving throw vs. paralyzation is also allowed. Success indicates that the bard recovered from his mistake without mishap.

Pipes of Haunting: When these powerful pipes are blown by a bard, those who fail their saving throws vs. spell are affected as if subject to a *fear* spell. Those who succeed on the roll still suffer the −2 penalty to morale checks and a −1 penalty to surprise rolls. The bard can choose to use the pipes normally.

Pipes of Pain: Because of the musical skills of bards, all within 60 feet are subject to the magic of these pipes when played by a bard. Saving throws are rolled with a −1 penalty per three levels of the bard.

Pipes of Sounding: Bards are able to generate any sound with these pipes, up to and including the volume of eight yelling men. The only limit is that the sound can't imitate any form of understandable verbal communication. Charlatans, however, can generate understandable communication.

Pipes of the Sewers: When played by bards, these pipes actually teleport the rats from some unknown location. Thus, a bard can summon rats even if he is in an area completely devoid of rats. Meistersingers can select whether giant or normal rats arrive, and have a +10% bonus to any control rolls.

Armor of Command: Bards wearing this armor are able to speak one command a day with the effects of the first level priest spell, *command*.

Sword of Dancing: Bards can release a *sword of dancing* on any round in which its plus isn't a 1 (*e.g.*, round 2,3,4,6,7,8, *etc.*). Blades of 5th level or higher can release the weapon after the first round; it will fight on its own for a number of rounds equal to the Blade's level before returning for one round.

Throughout History

This section contains a short, nonfantasy look at the history of music from the Dark Ages through the Renaissance period. This examination concentrates upon western culture, which is the primary basis for the AD&D® game.

Music was not always the sophisticated production that we of the 20th century are used to hearing. Although it has played a part in the life of the human race since before recorded history, modern music took many years to develop.

Before the time of the Christian church, music was rarely written down. With such sparse information, it is hard to decipher what the songs of the ancients were like. However, it is likely that they were very simple rhythms that were pounded out with sticks or simple percussion instruments.

Eventually reeds or canes were used to form the first woodwinds and a new musical sound emerged. But we still don't know what the music of this early era sounded like.

It wasn't until the 800s that music was being regularly recorded in western civilizations. Even then, it was only the monks of the Christian church who were writing it down. Thus, our records of these early songs are somewhat slanted. Music throughout most of the Dark Ages (up until A.D. 1100) consisted mainly of simple tunes that were played or sung in unison, thus they were pure melody (*i.e.*, no accompaniment). They were primarily used either to help pass time during work or to sing during religious ceremonies.

This Dark Age music was based on the modal scale, as opposed to the keyed scale of modern times. Dark Age music was likely borrowed from the Greeks and Romans. Although simple, it could be very elegant and beautifully expressive.

Near the end of the Dark Ages, musicians were combining several melodic lines. At first this was performed by mirroring a tune at a different pitch, but soon the added lines were taking on a form of their own, becoming a melody in their own right. This development was immeasurably enhanced when a system for writing down music developed around A.D. 900.

Around A.D. 1100, examples of written music begin appearing outside the Christian church. Songs and dances were written by and performed by public entertainers (like many of the bard kits included in this book). From the mid-14th century on, secular music was being composed and performed by professional musicians. However, such professionals were mainly employed by the church and a few nobles.

At the same time, music began to take on a more complicated form. Accompaniments and advanced multiple melodies (polyphonics) were being used. This spurred an increased demand for public entertainment and noblemen began taking a major interest in music. It became a matter of honor and pride for a nobleman to support a professional musician at his court.

During the Renaissance, the cry for secular music increased dramatically, with master compositions appearing around A.D. 1500. These compositions included both instrumental and vocal parts. Yet, even then, most composers wrote primarily for the church or wealthy noblemen.

Music continued to evolve through the baroque period (A.D. 1600–1750), classical period (A.D. 1750–1827), and on into the modern era, but these are beyond the scope of the AD&D® game.

Instruments

Most bards would not be caught dead without at least one musical instrument upon their person or near at hand. Many of their special abilities rely upon the use of an instrument. Instruments are also used as status symbols, trade symbols, and as part of the bard's per-

sonal garb. Some instruments take on a life of their own, gaining more fame than the bards who play them.

Musical instruments are very rare, expensive, and complicated devices. Only a master craftsmen would even think of constructing a lyre or herald's trumpet, let alone a pipe organ. Bards not only understand how these rare and complex devices work, they can use them to produce beautiful sounds. By simply working the strings and keys of these devices, bards can bring a crowd to tears or have them leaping for joy (all this without even using their kit's special benefits).

Most bardic colleges agree that the instruments of the time should be divide into four general categories: wind, stringed, percussion, and keyboard. Common instruments within each of these categories follow in Table 20 (as well as an "Other" category for several instruments that do not fall into the four general categories). After each instrument is a one-letter code that identifies the time period during which this instrument was developed and used; these periods coincide with the following dates.

Table 19: ERAS

Code	Era	Time Span
A	Ancient World	prior to A.D. 450
D	Dark Ages	A.D. 450–1100
M	Middle Ages	A.D. 1100–1450
R	Renaissance	A.D. 1450–1600

Musical Proficiency

There are now well over 50 musical instruments for bard players to choose from. Although such a large selection is nice, players might wonder if they have to spend a proficiency slot for each instrument they wish their bards to master. Fortunately, the answer is "no."

The instruments in Table 20 have been broken down into convenient categories and grouped appropriately into an indented outline format. A number in parenthesis appears after each level that contains subentries. This is the number of proficiency slots that must be spent in order to gain proficiency in *all* instruments indented beneath that level. For example, for five proficiency slots, a character can become proficient in all wind instruments; for only three slots he can limit himself to becoming proficient in all instruments in the flute family. Those instruments that don't have a number next to them cost a single slot to gain.

Note that proficiency in an instrument or category includes not only those instruments listed, but any others in his campaign world that fall into the same category. Thus, if a bard spends two slots to gain proficiency in bagpipes, he isn't limited to just the dudy and zampogna. He knows how to play any bagpipe that exists in his campaign world.

Cost and Weight

Note that some category names, such as "Bagpipes," are also the names of specific instruments. These categories have a gold piece cost and weight in pounds listed next to them so you can buy the instrument of that name. However, purchasing a generic bagpipe does not mean that you have both a dudy and zampogna—you have only a generic bagpipe.

Table 20: MUSICAL INSTRUMENTS

Instrument	Era Code	Cost (gp)	Wt (lb)
Wind (5)			
- Using holes or reeds (4)			
Bagpipes (2)	D	80	8
Dudy	D	75	8
Zampogna	D	85	8
Clarinet/Oboe family (3)	A	—	—
Aulos	R	35	2
Hautboy	M	30	2
Serpent	R	50	3
Shawm family (2)	A	—	—
Crumhorn	M	20	1
Curtall	M	25	1
Rackett	M	20	1
Shawm	D	15	1
Tibia	A	25	2
Flute family (3)	A	—	—
Fipple flute (2)	A	—	—
Bamboo pipe	A	5	1
Cornett	M	10	1
Double fipple	M	20	1
Flageolet	D	15	1
Nose flute	M	5	1
Recorder (1)	D	10	1
Gemshorn	A	5	2
Whistle flute (1)	A	5	.5
Penny	M	5	.5
Pipe	D	3	.5
Transverse flute (2)	A	—	—
Ocarina	A	15	1
Mouth Organ family (3)	A	—	—
Harmonica	A	5	.5
Khen	A	5	2
Panpipes	A	5	3
Sheng	A	5	3
Syrinx	A	5	2
- Using tubes and lips (4)			
Horn/Trumpet family (3)	A	—	—
Metal horns (2)	M	—	—
Coiled	M	65	5
Fanfare	M	35	4
Heralding	M	35	4

Instrument	Era Code	Cost (gp)	Wt (lb)
Posthorn	R	40	3
Slide	M	80	5
Straight	M	30	3
Nonmetal horns (2)	A	—	—
Alphorn	D	50	50
Animal horn	A	5	2
Conch shells	A	5	2
Hunting horns	D	10	3
Lur	A	5	1
Side horn	A	10	2
Trombone family (2)	M	—	—
Sackbut	M	95	12
Stringed (5)			
- Struck or plucked (4)			
Dulcimers (2)	M	60	15
Cimbalom	M	55	15
Cimbal	M	55	14
Psaltery	M	65	13
Santouri	M	60	15
Guitar family (3)	D	—	—
Balalaika	R	35	5
Citole	M	40	5
Cittern (1)	M	40	5
Pandora (Bass Cittern)	R	65	12
Bandora	R	45	6
Gittern	M	55	8
Lute (2)	D	35	4
Mandora	R	40	5
Shamisen	D	35	4
Sitar	M	40	4
Double-necked (1)	R	—	—
Chitarrone	R	65	8
Theorbo	R	70	8
Mandoline (mandolin)	M	40	5
Harp family (2)	A	75	8
AEolian harp	A	12	6
Clarsach	A	50	3
Lyre (1)	A	40	5
Crwth	D	35	4
Tallharpa	D	65	7

Instrument	Era Code	Cost (gp)	Wt (lb)	Instrument	Era Code	Cost (gp)	Wt (lb)
Zither family (2)	A	40	12	Cymbals	D	20	4
Ganun	A	35	12	Chimes	M	30	5
Koto	A	35	15	Gong (1)	D	20	35
				Tam-tam	D	20	35
- Bowed (4)				Triangle	D	5	1
Fiddle (2)	D	—	—				
Short-necked (1)	D	30	4	Clappers (1)	A	—	—
Lirica	M	30	4	Bones	A	1	1
Spiked	D	25	3	Castanets	M	2	1
				Claves	A	1	1
Hurdy gurdy (2)	M	80	8				
Organistrum	M	85	7	Rattle (1)	A	3	2
Rota	M	80	6	Gourds	A	2	2
				Sistrum	A	10	4
Rebec (2)	D	55	5				
Lira da braccio	M	65	8	Wooden Special Effects (2)	A	—	—
Lira da gamba	R	65	8	Clogs	D	2	.5
Lyra	D	55	6	Scraper	A	1	2
				Stamping stick	A	—	8
Tromba marina	D	15	7	Wooden block	A	1	1
Viol	M	70	8				
				Xylophone family (2)	A	—	—
Violin (2)	R	65	4	Glokenspiel	M	80	25
Kit	R	85	2	Metallophone	D	95	35
				Wooden Xylophone	A	60	20
Percussion (5)							
- With membranes (4)				**Keyboard (5)**			
Drums (3)	A	—	—	Clavichord (2)	R	500	150
Bongos	D	6	3				
Cylinder drums (2)	A	20	15	Harpsichord (3)	R	300	90
Changgo	A	25	10	Clavecin	R	275	85
Friction drums (2)	A	10	5	Clavicembalo	R	300	90
Gong drum	A	35	40	Spinet	R	275	85
Kettledrums (2)	A	30	30	Virginals	R	300	85
Nakers	M	35	25				
Tom-tom	D	30	30	Organ (3)	A	—	—
Side drums (2)	A	15	15	Hydraulis	A	250	100
Tabor	M	20	15	Positive organ	D	350	120
Slit drum	A	40	80	Pipe organ	M	1200	500
Talking drums (2)	A	30	20				
				Other (3)			
Tambourine (1)	A	5	2	Jew's harp	D	5	.5
Tambourine de provence	D	5	2	Kazoo	A	3	.5
				Nightingale	D	25	2
- Without membranes (4)				Sansa	A	5	4
Chime family (3)	A	—	—				
Bells	A	25	3				

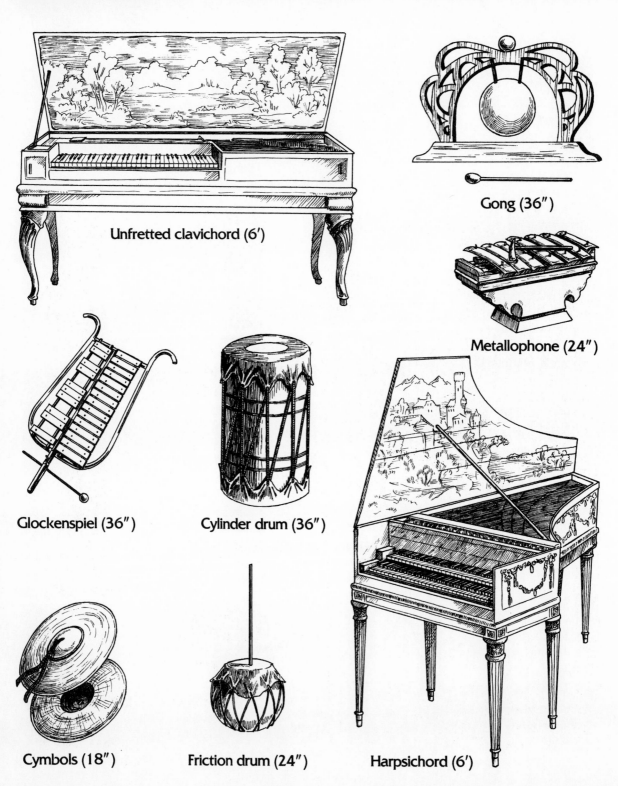

Unfretted clavichord (6')

Gong (36")

Metallophone (24")

Glockenspiel (36")

Cylinder drum (36")

Cymbols (18")

Friction drum (24")

Harpsichord (6')

Clapper bell (8″)

Pellet bell (4″)

Castinets (3″)

Tamborine (12″)

Pipe organ (8′)

Temple bell
with subsidiary bells
as clappers (24″)

Gourd rattle (12″)

Gourd rattle (24″)

Sistrum (18″)

Dulcimer (hackbrett)
and beaters (24″)

Hunting horn,
ivory & silver (24″)

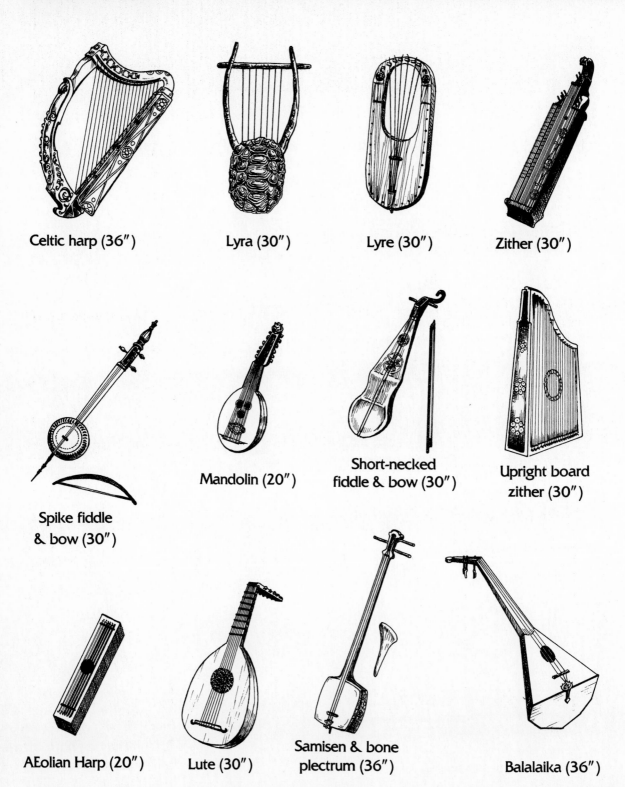

Celtic harp (36")

Lyra (30")

Lyre (30")

Zither (30")

Spike fiddle
& bow (30")

Mandolin (20")

Short-necked
fiddle & bow (30")

Upright board
zither (30")

Æolian Harp (20")

Lute (30")

Samisen & bone
plectrum (36")

Balalaika (36")

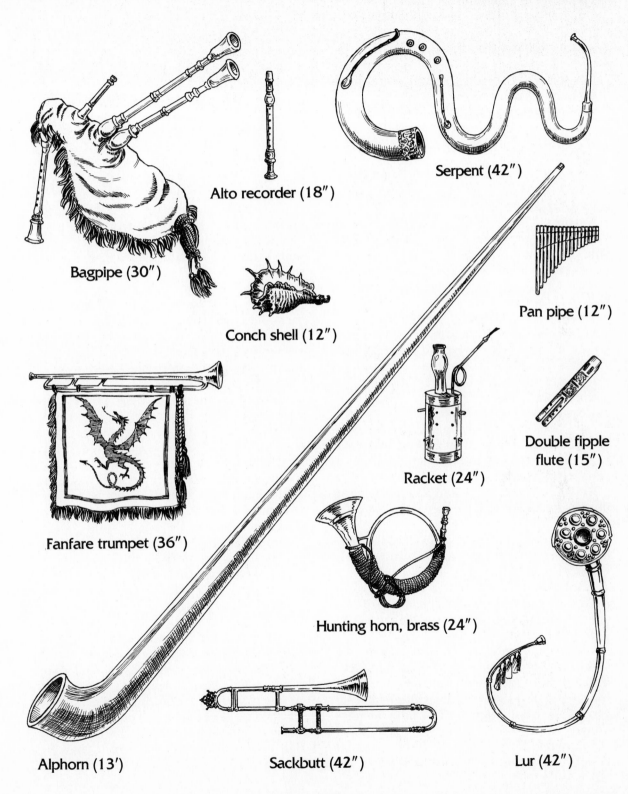

Bagpipe (30")

Alto recorder (18")

Serpent (42")

Conch shell (12")

Pan pipe (12")

Fanfare trumpet (36")

Racket (24")

Double fipple flute (15")

Hunting horn, brass (24")

Alphorn (13')

Sackbutt (42")

Lur (42")

Glossary of Musical Instruments

The following section describes some of the aforementioned musical instruments.

AEolian harp: Named after the Greek god of winds, this instrument is played by the wind. AEolian harps resemble flat boxes with strings.

Alphorn: An alphorn is a 6- to 12-foot-long, "J"-shaped, Swiss horn used to call cattle, among other things.

Bagpipe: This ancient instrument was used throughout the world: Rome, Northumberland, Scotland, Ireland, Brittany, France, Italy, Spain, Portugal, Norway, Finland, Poland, Russia, Greece, Persia, China, India, and the Balkan countries.

Balalaika: This is a three-string Russian triangular guitar. It comes in various sizes, the largest resting upon the ground when played.

Bells: These are sometimes attached to clothing to accentuate rhythm in dance.

Bones: A simple instrument in which two pieces of bone are clacked together.

Castanets: This Spanish instrument consists of two small, hollow-shaped pieces of wood. Castanets are worn on the finger and thumb. Like bones, they are clacked together.

Cembalo: This was the old Italian name for dulcimer (but it was later used to refer to the harpsichord).

Chitarrone: This double-necked lute is very large, often six feet long, and has 20 wires. It was also called the Roman theorbo.

Citole: This instrument was invented in Italy. It has a flat body, a short neck, four brass or steel strings, and is plucked with a quill. By 1550 this was known as the cittern.

Cittern: A member of the guitar family, the cittern is shaped like a fig, with a flat back, fretted fingerboard, and wire strings (usually four pairs). It is a descendant of the Medieval citole. The bass cittern is also called the pandora.

Clappers: Two pieces of hard material (wood, bone, metal, *etc.*) struck together are called clappers. They have existed for thousands of years in all parts of world (as spoons, bones, *etc.*).

Clarsach: An ancient small harp of the Scottish highlands.

Clavecin: French harpsichord.

Claves: When these short, round sticks of hardwood are used, the hollow of one's hand acts as a resonating cavity for sound amplification.

Clavicembalo: This is the Italian harpsichord and is often abbreviated as "cembalo." The word derives from latin "clavis"—a key, and "cembalo"—a dulcimer, which describes the instrument—it's a keyed dulcimer.

Clavichord: This keyboard instrument is small, often just an oblong box placed on the table. It can have its own legs and stand on the floor, but this was a later development. Sound is made when a small piece of metal hits a string, producing a soft, quiet tone.

Clogs: Wooden shoes.

Cornett: The cornett (not cornet) is a woodwind with a cupped mouthpiece (like that of a trumpet) that comes in three sizes: treble, small treble, and tenor. It is shaped either as a straight tube or as a tube curved like an S.

Crumhorn: This double-reed woodwind comes in all sizes: trebles, tenors, and basses.

Cymbals: These are brass dishes that are slammed together.

Drums: Drums have existed for thousands of years. The many types have one thing in common: a skin or membrane stretched tightly over some kind of hollow vessel. The membrane is beaten with sticks or the hands.

The exception is the friction drum, which has its skin pierced by a stick or string that is rubbed or pulled, causing the skin to vibrate.

Kettledrums are metal bowls with parchment stretched over them.

Side drums are wooden or metal cylinders with skin over each end. The lower end has string or gut, called snares, stretched over it that causes the drum to rattle when it is beaten.

Bass drums are very large, double-headed drums from two to three feet in diameter and of equal length.

Gong drums are like bass drums but they have only one head (membrane).

Bongos are two small drums that sit side by side.

Tom-toms are small Oriental drums with pigskin heads stretched over a bowl-shaped shell.

Cylinder drums are a type of base drum that is beaten at both ends.

The *changgo* is a Korean two-headed lap drum.

Talking drums are used to send messages.

Slit drums can be made by hollowing out a tree or log through a long narrow slit. The wood is then beaten to produce the sound.

Dulcimer: Used in Hungary, Rumania, and Czechoslovakia, the dulcimer is a shallow, closed box over which are strung wires that are struck with a wooden hammer. In Hungary and Rumania this is called a cimbalom, and in Greece, a santouri.

Fanfare trumpet: This is often hung with a heraldic banner and used for state and ceremonial purposes.

Fiddle: There are two types of fiddles: folk (or spiked) fiddles and medieval fiddles. A spiked fiddle is a type of bowed lute and either has a long neck (typical of Africa, Asia, and the Middle East) or a short neck as found in Europe. Most spiked fiddles have one to three strings.

Medieval fiddles were replaced by the viol family and usually had three to five strings with both flat and rounded backs.

Fipple flute: This type of flute is held vertically and is winded from the end.

Flute: There are two types of flutes: the vertically winded fipple flute and the horizontally held transverse flute. The transverse is made of wood or metal stopped at one end. The player blows in a side hole, with notes made by closing holes along the flute's body.

Gemshorn: This is an ancient type of recorder made of chamois or goat horn.

Gittern: A medieval guitar.

Glokenspiel: This originated in Germany and was used in war bands.

Gong: A gong is a large metal plate that is struck with a mallet.

Harmonica: This instrument originated in Asia and China around 1100 B.C.

Harp: The harp is an ancient instrument. It consists of a sound box near the player and numerous strings that are each plucked to produce a specific tone.

Harpsichord: This is much like a keyboarded psaltery in that its keys cause the string to be plucked.

Horns: Horns have existed all over the world throughout recorded history. The earliest form was the animal horn or large sea shell. Most are end-blown, but some side-blown horns exist. Metal horns arose in the 14th century and were made of brass, copper, and occasionally silver. They were slender tubes 6 to 12 feet long, often coiled in several circles with a flared bell.

Hurdy gurdy: This mechanical instrument resembles a viola with a handle to crank. Cranking it causes a wheel to revolve under its four to six strings like an endless bow. A small keyboard is used to silence certain strings.

Jew's harp: This instrument is called a feugdtromp (child's trumpet) by the Dutch. It has no connection to the Jewish religion. It is a bottle-shaped wire frame with metal tongue held in teeth, allowing the mouth cavity to alter the sound it produces.

Kazoo: Although considered a humorous instrument today, the kazoo is of ancient origin.

Kit: A small violin.

Koto: The most famous Japanese instrument is the 13-stringed Japanese zither known as the koto. The instrument is played on the ground or while resting on a low table.

Lira da braccio, lira da gamba: These are Italian stringed instruments. The lira da braccio has seven strings and is played like a violin.

The lira da gamba is a bass instrument held between the knees and has 11 to 16 strings.

Lur: The lur is an ancient trumpet of Scandinavian origin. It is made in pairs twisting in opposite directions to resemble horns or the tusks of an animal.

Lute: The lute is of Persian-Arabian origin and came to Europe at the time of the crusades. The body resembles a pear split lengthwise. Thus, it has a curved back, a flat belly, and a fretted neck. It ranges in size from the large chitarrone and theorbo to the small mandora.

Lyre: The lyre has existed since 3000 BC. It has four components: a sound box, two arms, and a crossbar. Strings run from the cross bar down across the sound box.

Mandoline or mandolin: A lute-shaped, small stringed instrument.

Metallophone: This resembles a xylophone, but it has metal bars that are beaten with small hammers.

Nakers: These are small kettledrums of Arabian origin that came west during the crusades. They are made of metal or wooden bowls covered with skin and are used in pairs like bongos.

Nightingale: This toy whistle of glass is lowered into water to emit a bubbling sound not unlike the nightingale (*i.e.*, the bird).

Ocarina: This vessel flute is globular or pear-shaped with a mouthpiece on one side and holes cut in its body. The holes are opened and closed with the fingers.

Organ: An organ has pipes connected to a wind supply that is controlled by a keyboard. There are two types of organ pipes: flue pipes and reed pipes. Flue pipes produce sound like a whistle-flute. Reed pipes contain a thin strip of metal that vibrates. Organ pipes range from lengths of a few inches to 64 feet.

If an organ is keyed with the hands it is called a "manual," if played with the feet it is a "pedal boards."

Pandora or Bandora: This is the bass cittern; it has a flat back with wire strings and frets. It usually has three pronounced ridges, making it easy to identify.

Panpipes: Panpipes are simply a set of whistle-flutes supposedly invented by the god Pan.

Posthorn: A posthorn was used to announce the arrival of a mail coach. Most were straight, although a few were coiled.

Psaltery: This type of dulcimer has a square or triangular box over which are strings. It is held on the lap or against the chest and plucked.

Rackett: This is an early double-reed woodwind.

Rattle: A rattle can be made of a gourd, clay, wood, or leather, and it is filled with pellets.

Rebec: This is the stringed ancestor of the violin family. The rebec evolved from the Arabian fiddle but has a rounded back, unlike the fiddle. The body is pear shaped and has three strings. The rebec is played on the shoulder or against the chest.

Recorder: Also known as the English flute, the recorder is blown at the end. It has eight holes with which to alter the produced sound.

Sansa: The sansa is African in origin and has a metal or cane tongue attached to a wooden board or box. It is also called the thumb piano.

Scraper: When you scrape a stick over a series of notches in wood or bone, you have a basic scraper.

Serpent: This woodwind is shaped like a pronounced S.

Shamisen (samisen): This Japanese long-necked lute has a square wooden body. Its belly and bottom are made of cat skin and it has frets with three strings that are plucked hard.

Shawm: This early double-reed is an outdoor instrument that produces a loud buzzing sound.

Sheng: This is a Chinese mouth organ.

Sistrum: The sistrum is an open, U-shaped rattle that contains metal discs or other objects that rattle when shaken.

Sitar: This three- to seven-stringed Indian lute was invented in Persia.

Stamping stick: One of the oldest known instruments is the stamping stick. It is simply a length of hollow wood or bamboo that is beaten on the ground. It was often used to beat grain or other food into pulp while providing simple music during work.

Tabor: This early side (snare) drum is usually slung from the waist. Smaller versions can be played with just the left hand while the bard plays a small whistle flute in the other hand.

Tambourine: The tambourine likely originated in Rome. It is a shallow wooden hoop parchment stretched over a frame that is struck with knuckles or rubbed with the thumb. The hoop has imbedded metal plates that jingle when shaken.

Tam-tam: Bronze gong of Chinese origin.

Theorbo: A double-necked instrument.

Triangle: A triangle is a steel bar bent into a triangle that is struck with a metal rod.

Trumpet: The Medieval trumpet was non-valved and was played from the side or end.

Violin: This instrument evolved from the fiddle, rebec, and lira da braccio.

Viols and Viol family: These instruments produce a soft sound; they resemble violins. However, their shoulders slope, their backs are flat, their sound holes are C-shaped, they have broader necks, and they have six strings, not four.

Wood block: A Chinese percussion instrument made of a hollow wooden block that is struck with a stick.

Zither: The zither has a flat box that is strung with strings of metal or gut. It is plucked while resting on a table.

Xylophone: This consists of hardwood blocks that are hit with a mallet.

Glossary of Sound

Although a degree in music isn't required to play a bard character, it often increases realism if such players know a few basics. This way they can role-play their characters with an air of authority, understanding, and authenticity. For this reason, a few common terms associated with many forms of music are defined below. By briefly studying this mini-glossary, you can breathe some new life into the vocabulary of your bard.

Fundamentals of Music

Accent: To stress or emphasize a note.

Type	Stressed by
Dynamic	Volume
Tonic	Pitch
Agogic	Value (see *Value*)

Beat: Unit of measure that sets the tempo. Beats are measured by tapping one's foot, the stroke of the conductor's baton, *etc.*

Compass: The range of a voice or instrument.

Dynamics: The gradations of loudness or softness with which music is performed.

Term	Meaning
Pianissimo	very soft
Piano	soft
Mezzo piano	moderately soft
Mezzo forte	moderately loud
Forte	loud
Fortissimo	very loud
Forte piano	loud, then soft
Sforzando, sforzato	sharply accented
Forzando, forzato	sharply accented
Crescendo	gradually louder
Decrescendo	gradually softer
Diminuendo	gradually softer

Form: Musical structure and how the musical elements are put together. The basic elements are individual pitches (notes), how they sound together (harmony), and how much time they take up in relation to one another (rhythm).

Frequency: Sound wave crests per second, which determines pitch.

Intonation: A performer's accuracy with respect to pitch.

Measure or bar: The base grouping of beats (usually there are 2, 3, or 4 beats per measure).

Melody: A group of musical tones in sequence making up a meaningful whole.

Meter: The number of beats per measure and the type of note that defines a beat. Common meters are 2/2 (two beats based on half notes), 2/4 (two beats based on quarter notes), 3/4 (three beats based on quarter notes), and 4/4 (four beats based on quarter notes).

Motion: The musical pattern created by successive notes. The motion might rise and fall smoothly or jump around.

Pitch: The highness or lowness of a musical tone. Pitch is determined by a note's frequency.

Range: The entire series of notes (from lowest to highest) that a voice or instrument can produce.

Rhythm: The movement of musical tones with respect to time. Rhythm combines the aspects of tempo (speed) and value (length of notes).

Style: The manner in which music is treated. A few of the numerous stylistic directives and their meanings are listed below.

Style	Meaning
Affabile	smoothly and graceful
Affettuoso	tenderly with feeling
Agilmente	lightly and smoothly
Agitato	restlessly, in an excited manner
Angstlich	fearfully, in an anxious manner
Animato	lively, in a spirited manner
Appasionato	with intense feeling
Brillante	in a showy, brilliant manner

Brusco	abruptly, with harsh accents

Tempo: The speed at which a piece is played or sung.

Tempos	Order of Speed
Adagissimo	Very slow
Largo	
Lento	
Adagio	
Adagietto	
Andante or Moderato	Moderate
Andantino	
Allegretto	
Allegro	
Presto	Very fast

Changing Tempos	Meaning
Allentando	Slow down
Ritardando	Gradually slow down
Rallentando	Gradually slow down
Allargando	Slow down and play louder
Rubato	Free tempo
Accelerando	Gradually speed up
Calcando	Speed up

Tone: Any sound of definite pitch. Also refers to the quality of sound.

Value: The duration of a note.

Voice Range: Range of voice. Each bard can be classified as one of the following:

Voice	Range
Soprano	Highest female range
Mezzo soprano	Mid female range
Alto	Lowest female range, highest male range
Tenor	High male range
Baritone	Mid male range
Bass	Lowest male range

Volume: Loudness.

Common Musical Terms

Accompaniment: Musical material that supports the main melody or voice-part.

Arrangement: Rewriting of a composition for a new medium (instrument, voice, group).

Concert: A public performance of music other than opera or church music.

Conducting: The art of directing a group of musical performers.

Conservatory or College: A school that specializes in musical instruction.

Debut: First public performance of a musician.

Encore: Audience's appeal for an additional performance.

Movement: A major section in a song.

Notation: A system for writing down music using notes.

Musical Groups:

Group Composition:

Group	Components
Band	Brass, woodwind, & percussion
Choir	Group of singers
Chorus	Large choir having more than one singer per part
Ensemble	Any group of performers
Orchestra	Stringed, brass, woodwind, and percussion

Group Size:

Name	Number of voices or instruments
Solo	1
Recital	1 or 2
Duet	2
Trio	3
Quartet	4
Quintet	5
Sextet	6
Septet	7
Octet	8
Nonet	9

Part: The music written for a single type of instrument.

Passage: Any short section of a musical composition.

Score: The written notes to be performed by all instruments or voices.

Tuning: Adjusting an instrument so it produces the proper sounds.

Musical Items

Baton: The slender stick used by conductors to direct a performance.

Metronome: A device that produces regularly timed beats.

Mute: A device that muffles the sound of an instrument.

Plectrum: General name for any device used to pluck the strings of a musical instrument.

Podium: Raised platform on which the conductor stands.

Types of Songs

Air de cour: A short song of several stanzas for one or more voices accompanied by lute or harpsichord.

Anthem: A short choral piece based on a religious text or source.

Arabesque: A short imaginative piece.

Aria: An elaborate solo song generally with instrumental accompaniment.

Arioso: A style of recitative that is more song-like and expressive than ordinary recitative.

Aubade: A piece of instrumental music played in the morning as opposed to the serenade, which is played in the evening.

Ayre: An English solo song accompanied by the lute, theorbo, or bass viol (and occasionally by two singers).

Bagatelle: A short piece for a keyboard instrument.

Ballad: A solo song that tells a story in simple verse. The same music is repeated for each stanza.

Bandinerie: A fast, dancelike piece.

Canon or Fugue: A musical composition in which a melody in one voice-part is imitated by other voice-parts that are slightly offset (*e.g.*, row, row, row your boat).

Carol, Noel, or Weihnachtslied: A song sung in honor of a holiday (*e.g.*, Christmas songs).

Chant: Usually refers to the music of churches.

Fa-la: An English song sung in nonsense syllables (*e.g.*, falala, fa la la).

Fanfare: A tune used to announce someone's arrival, the start of a parade, the start of a jousting tournament, *etc.*

Folk music: Music that is learned by word of mouth.

Hymn: Any song that expresses praise or love of a deity.

Improvisation: Composing a song or theme as it is being performed.

Jig: A lively dance.

Lai: A form of music and poetry developed in France in the 13th Century.

Lament: A composition that mourns someone's death.

Lullaby: A cradle song used by mothers to lull their babies to sleep.

Lyric: Means "songlike." Often used to describe instrumental pieces that are short and expressive.

Medley: A group of familiar tunes played one after another and loosely linked together.

National anthem: A song adopted by a kingdom as its official song.

Ode: A musical setting of a poem written in honor of a person or special occasion.

Opera: A play in which the characters sing rather than speak.

Parody: An exaggerated imitation of a composition, often to make fun of it.

Program music: A general term for music that tells a story.

Psalm: A musical composition based on the text from the book of Psalms.

Recitative: A style of singing that closely resembles speech, with little change in pitch and rhythm.

Round: A vocal composition with three or more parts that enter one after another, repeating the same words (*e.g.*, canons and fugues).

Serenade: A love song sung during the evening below a beloved's window.

Shanty: A work song sung by sailors to help keep time during jobs that require teamwork.

Swan song: A term used for a person's final work before his death.

Sample Songs

The following are a few sample songs to whet your appetite. If you would like to write your own songs for your bard to sing, it is suggested that you get a book of old, traditional folk songs, and replace existing words with those of your own choosing.

Bonnie George Campbell (Scottish ballad)

1. Hie upon Hielands, and laigh upon Tay,
Bonnie George Campbell rode out on a day.
He saddled, he bridled, and gallant rode he,
And hame cam his guid horse, but never cam he.

2. Out cam his mother, dear, greeting fu sair,
And out cam his bonnie bryde, riving her hair.
The meadow lies green, the corn is unshorn,
But bonnie George Campbell will never return.

3. Saddled and bridled and booted rode he,
A plume in his helmet, a sword at his knee.
But toom cam his saddle, all bloody to see,
Oh, hame cam his guid horse, but never cam he!

My Gentle Harp (Irish love song)

1. My gentle harp, once more I waken
the sweetness of thy slumb'ring strain,
In tears our last farewell was taken,
And now in tears we meet again.
Yet even then while peace was singing
Her halcyon song o'er land and sea,
Though joy and hope to others bringing,
She only brought new tears to thee.

2. Then who can ask for notes of pleasure,
My drooping harp, from chords like thine?
Alas, the lark's gay morning measure
As ill would suit the swan's decline.
Or how shall I, who love, who bless thee,
Invoke thy breath for freedom's strains,

When e'en the wreaths in which I dress thee,
Are sadly mixed, half flowers, half chains?

Skye Boat Song (Scottish ballad)

1. Loud the winds howl, loud the waves roar
Thunder clouds rend the air;
Baffled our foe's stand on the shore,
Follow they will not dare.

2. Though the waves leap, soft shall ye sleep,
Ocean's a royal bed;
Rock'd in the deep, Flora will keep
watch by your weary head.

3. Many's the lad fought on that day,
Well the claymore could wield
When the night came, silently lay
Dead on Culloden's field.

4. Burn'd our homes, exile and death
Scatter the loyal men;
Yet, e'er the sword cool in the sheath,
Charlie will come again.

Chorus:
Speed, bonnie boat, like a bird on the wing,
"Onward!" the sailors cry.
"Carry the lad that's born to be king
Over the sea to Skye!"

The Minstrel Boy (Irish song of valor)

1. The minstrel boy to the war is gone,
In the ranks of death you'll find him;
His father's sword he has girded on,
And his wild harp slung behind him.
"Land of song!" said the warrior bard,
"Though all the world betrays thee,
One sword, at least, thy rights shall guard,
One faithful harp shall praise thee."

2. The minstrel fell, but the foeman's chain
Could not bring that proud soul under;
The harp he lov'd ne'er spoke again,
For he tore its chords a sunder;
And said, "No chain shall sully thee,
Thou soul of love and bravery
Thy songs were made for the pure and free,
They shall never sound in slavery."

A Bard's Mind Isn't Barred

Welcome to the mind of a bard. To play a bard, you must think like a bard. He is a dreamer, a romantic, and a part-time philosopher. A bard wants to be a master of all skills. He wants to try everything, know everything, and be everything. Unfortunately, most bards are mortal. The constraints of mortality keep a bard moving from one profession and activity to the next. He fears that if he spends too much time in one place or doing one thing, he will miss out on something else.

Pragmatists claim that bards suffer from "green pasture syndrome." This syndrome gets its name from cows. They constantly poke their heads over or through fences in an attempt to eat the grass on the other side. Farmers laugh at their livestock because the grass in their own pasture is often greener than the grass on the other side. But the cows have green pasture syndrome and always seem to think that things are better somewhere else.

Bards are easily excited about new developments, upcoming events, and change in general. If things aren't changing, they become bored very quickly. Thus, bards are not ones to hold down long-time jobs. When they do take jobs, they work at them at a breakneck pace at first. Then, as the job becomes routine, their pace slows and they spend more time pondering the future and where it will take them next.

All of this is also true for adventuring bards. They want to get going, attack now, stop listening at every door, rush forward and meet life head on. Bards don't always select the most effective spells or the most advantageous proficiencies. Instead, they select the most dramatic, the most fun, those that can be used in unique situations. A flashy spell, such as *color spray*, is always preferable to a boring one, such as *hold portal* or *sleep*.

Bards love crowds and love to be around people. They tend to have many acquaintances but few close friends. Some bards actually push away those who try to get too close. A binding friendship or relationship is like a root: It attempts to plant the bard in one place and lock him into the relationship. This is far more than just undesirable to most bards—it is downright frightening. Bards enjoy their freedom and don't want anything to jeopardize it.

Of all the character classes, none are as carefree and lighthearted as bards. These characters rarely own more than they can carry. To bards, all the world is their home and their imagination is the only limit to their aspirations. Although they can be profoundly moved by others' plights, bards recover quickly from any sadness they might feel. Often they deal with problems by leaving them behind and traveling on to some greener pasture.

If you are going to play a bard, remember at least this one rule of thumb: Your character's main goal is to, "move on and experience all that there is."

Experience

According to the *Dungeon Master's Guide* (Chapter 2: Experience), bards gain experience for the following reasons:

Table 21: BARD EXPERIENCE

XP	Reason
200	Per successful use of a special ability
2	Per gold piece value of treasure obtained
5	Per hit die of creatures defeated
Typ*	Monster experience
Typ*	Other group experience

*"Typ" stands for a typical share of experience.

All of the above reasons are self-explanatory except for "successful use of a special ability." A bard's special abilities include his thief skills, his ability to read any

written magical item, and his special benefits.

If you would like to tailor experience awards to better reflect the experiences of the bard class, the following is suggested.

Table 22: COMPLETE BARD EXPERIENCE

XP	Reason
100	Per successful use of a thief ability
200	Per successful use of 10th-level ability to read any written magical device
150	Per successful use of a special benefit
25	Per spell level cast to overcome foes or problems
100	For each significant performance of the bard's entertaining talents
500	For each major performance of the bard's entertaining talents
1	Per gold piece value of treasure obtained
5	Per hit die of creatures defeated
Typ*	Monster experience
Typ*	Other group experience

*"Typ" stands for a typical share of experience.

Reputation

So how good is a bard's performance? It depends partly upon his skill and level, but most importantly, upon his reputation. The songs of a famous skald hailing from the icy north are met with great anticipation and acceptance. An infamous blade known for his many assassinations draws just as large a crowd to his daring performances of weaponry.

Reputation is an intangible aspect of any bard. As the bard travels the path of life, his reputation can grow into that of a great singing hero, it can be slandered so everyone thinks the bard is a cowardly oaf, or the bard's reputation can become an infamous cloak with which to frighten watchmen and thrill the crowds.

When you first generate your character, his reputation is based upon that of his family. From there, events and the way the bard is role-played continually adjust his reputation. Read on for the events that define a bard's reputation.

Following a Performer

A bard's reputation is a variable that can change in an instant. Furthermore, reputation varies from one village or town to the next. A bard's initial reputation applies to his home town only. This is the center of the bard's reputation.

Let's follow the development of the great Hanalacious's reputation. She put on her first public performance in Greyhawk City at the age of 16. First impressions are extremely important and vary uncontrollably depending upon the mood of the audience, season, local events, *etc*. After her first performance, Hana became a "noted" member of the entertaining class.

To determine Hana's initial reputation, the following table was consulted.

Table 23: INITIAL REPUTATION

2d4 Roll	Index	Title
2	0	Unsung
3	1	Accepted
4	2	Known
5	3	Noted
6	4	Good standing
7	5	Liked
8	6	Well-known

Hanalacious was pleased with her initial reputation, but she had aspirations of greatness. She looked upon those great bards who were her teachers, and she envied the reputations they had built for themselves. Some were popular, some were celebrated, a few were even acclaimed by the citizens of Greyhawk, but Hana wanted to attain a revered reputation for herself.

Table 24: REPUTATION LADDER

Index	Title
0	Unsung
1	Accepted
2	Known
3	Noted
4	Good standing
5	Liked
6	Well-known
7	Admired
8	Prominent
9	Distinguished
10	Popular
11	Reputable
12	Honored
13	Celebrated
14	Illustrious
15	Eminent
16	Acclaimed
17	Prestigious
18	Famous/Infamous
19	Renowned
20	Revered

Table 25: REPUTATION MODIFIERS

Last performance was:	
within the week	+1
over a week ago	+0
over a month ago	−1
over 3 months ago	−2
over 6 months ago	−3
over 9 months ago	−4
over a year ago	−5
Each attempt to publicly influence reactions	
that succeeds	+2
fails but no reaction adjustment	−1
fails and worsens reactions	−3
Money spent on local appearance/reputation:	
0% of income	−2
10% of income	+0
25% of income	+1
50% of income	+2
75% of income	+3
90% of income	+4
Completed a local adventure	+1
Fulfilled a local quest	+2
Blamed for a violent crime	−2
Convicted of a violent crime	−5
DM's option	+/−5

Reaching for a revered reputation would be a long and delicate process for Hanalacious. She would have to watch her every action and word, being careful to avoid entanglements with the law, yet helping those in need. Of course, all this would mean nothing if she didn't also put on frequent performances of her musical talents.

Hana made a list of all the things that could both help and hinder her climb to fame on the ladder in Table 24. Among them she included the following:

Hanalacious realized that there are two types of reputable performers, both of whom draw large crowds: those who are famous and those who are infamous. The famous person is looked upon as a public hero, upholder of good, and a generally law-abiding citizen. The infamous performer is well known as a courser, a romantic thief who lives above the law and leads a high-paced, romantic life (*e.g.*, Robin Hood).

Of course, Hana decided to walk the path to infamy, realizing that there is a huge gap between an infamous performer and a violent bully, ruthless thug, or evil villain.

Again, Hana made a list of those actions that gained a person the reputation of being infamous as opposed to those that gained a person fame.

Table 26: FAME AND INFAMY

Fame Scale:

Calmed a violent situation	+2
Made a hostile person look foolish	+1
Turned a crowd's mood against evil	+3
Prevented a crime from occurring	+2
Upheld a good person's reputation	+1
Upheld what's right vs. adversaries	+1

Infamy Scale:

Blamed for a nonviolent crime	+1
Avoided imprisonment	+2
Escaped imprisonment	+3
Make town watch look foolish	+1
Created a political scandal	+3

For a bard trying to become infamous, performing acts on the infamy list improve the chances for building his reputation, while performing acts on the fame scale decrease these chances. The opposite is true for a bard who is attempting to become famous.

A bard's reputation is adjusted only in two situations: when he increases in level, and when he puts on a significant public performance (in which case it is checked just as the performance begins).

A d20 is rolled and any modifiers from the preceding three tables are applied to it only if their total is negative (if the net total modifier ends up being positive, it is simply ignored).

If the result of the d20, adjusted by a possible negative modifier, is greater than or equal to the bard's current reputation, then the reputation increases one category. If the net result is a negative number, the bard's reputation is lowered by this amount (thus a net result of −3 would lower the bard's reputation by three places on Table 24). If the roll falls in between, nothing happens. However, no matter what, a natural roll of 20 always increases the

bard's reputation by 1 and a natural roll of 1 always decreases it by at least 1 (more if there are negative modifiers).

No matter what the roll, all reputation modifiers reset afterward, and the bard once again has a net 0 adjustment.

Eventually, Hanalacious became infamously acclaimed (16) in Greyhawk City, but she felt stilted by performing for the same crowd over and over gain. What she wanted was a fresh audience; one that had heard of her infamous reputation, but that hadn't been to any of her performances. Thus, she contacted the bard college, known as the Society of the Silver Lute, in the nearby town of Hardby. She had several of the college's members advertise that the Infamous Hanalacious would soon be performing for the public.

Two weeks later, Hana arrived in Hardby. She was pleased to note that her reputation had somewhat preceded her. She wasn't acclaimed (16) like she was in Greyhawk City, but she was treated as an illustrious (14) personality. Of course, the distance from her established Greyhawk City base was responsible for the slight decline. The following table shows the decline in reputation as a bard moves away from his base, where he has an established reputation.

Table 27: PRECEDING REPUTATION

Distance from base	Reputation Decline
1 town or 25 miles	−2
2 towns or 50 miles	−4
3 towns or 100 miles	−6
4 towns or 150 miles	−8
5 towns or 200 miles	−10
Farther	No reputation

Local Reputation

As noted earlier, a bard's initial reputation applies to his home town only. This reputation increases and decreases based upon repu-

tation modifiers. Furthermore, the decision whether to become infamous or famous must be made. This selection determines how certain events affect the bard's reputation.

When a bard enters another village, town, or city, his reputation should be determined for that area. This is done by consulting Table 27. The bard's closest established reputation is used as a base. An established reputation is defined as a place in which the bard has put on some form of entertainment performance. The closest established reputation is then adjusted by distance.

For example, if the nearest established reputation is two towns away, the bard's local reputation is four levels lower. If the bard wishes to establish a local reputation, he simply puts on a public performance or series of performances (spread out over no more than a year's time). Each performance costs the bard 100 gp per 1,000 citizens in the town (*i.e.*, 1 silver piece per person). The bard then becomes an established performer in the community.

Once a reputation is established, it is never again influenced by other established reputations. Thus, after Hanalacious's big performance in Hardby, her reputation in Greyhawk City has no impact upon her reputation in Hardby. She thus has an independent, established reputation in both cities. Hana's player should write down the two city names and note Hana's reputation next to each name.

Benefits of a Good Reputation

Reputation is treated much like a special proficiency, although no proficiency slots are (or can be) spent on it. When a situation arises in which the bard's reputation should be considered, 1d20 is rolled—this is called a reputation check. Any roll equal to or less than the bard's reputation level is considered a success. However, no such roll should ever replace role-playing. In fact, the bard player should role-play any situation before a reputation check is made. The Dungeon Master should

then assign an adjustment to the reputation check based upon the role-playing.

If a bard is attempting to alter encounter reactions (*i.e.*, influence reactions or some similar ability), a successful reputation check indicates that the bard can adjust the reactions by two levels instead of the typical one.

A reputation can be used as an invisible key. A successful reputation check can get a bard into private parties or functions even when the bard isn't on the guest registry. A reputable bard will also find it easy to get a seat at the most prominent banquet hall in town, even if there is a long line and the bard failed to make a reservation.

Dealing with prominent public figures is also easier with a good reputation. A city's mayor is more likely to invite a reputable person to dinner than a commoner. Reputation can also be used to help smooth out deals, such as the price required to rent the public theater for a weekend's performance.

Many other uses of reputation exist and should be adjudicated by the Dungeon Master.

The Performer

So what is it that makes bards such fantastic entertainers? Why is a bard with a 15 proficiency in musical instrument any better than a fighter, priest, or wizard with a 15? What makes bards so special? The answer to these questions and other questions are found in this section.

Unlike all the other character classes, bards are performers. This is a special trait common to all bards. There is no die roll bonus associated with this trait, it isn't listed under any kit's special benefits, and it isn't a proficiency.

Being a true performer is so fundamental to the bard character class that it isn't listed at all. Instead, this fact influences almost every aspect of the character class. It is because of their performing nature that bards gain special abilities with music, song, poems, jug-

gling, and so on (based upon the kit). Being performers is as fundamental to the bard class as being combatants is to the warrior class. It is the one element common to all the bard kits, the element that defines the essence of being a bard.

Back to the example of musical instrument proficiency. It is true that a warrior with a proficiency of 16 in musical instruments is able to play more precisely and more accurately than a bard with a 15 or less. However, playing music technically correct is only half the picture. Since bards are performers, they understand numerous hidden aspects relating to music. They are more in tune with their audience and adapt their performances appropriately. Bards are more aware of mood, feeling, tone, and the dramatic effects of stretching the music beyond the technicalities of precise playing.

A warrior who is a master musician (proficiency 20) can play the most complicated piece of music exactly as written. Moreover, every time he plays the piece, it sounds just as it did the last time. But a bard with only a 15 proficiency can entertain audiences far more successfully. Every performance is custom tailored to the occasion and the audience. The bard takes the liberty of interpreting the song and won't simply repeat it.

The Effect on Role-Playing

As a role-player, if you can capture this performing aspect of the bard class, you will have captured the essence of your character. Everything should center around this aspect. The spells you choose should not always be chosen to maximize your character's effectiveness in combat. Rather, they should make the most dramatic impact upon those around him (including the adventuring party). Your bard lives to perform.

Likewise, when you select your bard's weapons, clothing, items, proficiencies, friends, allies, enemies, *etc.*, you should try to

examine these choices from a performer's point of view.

What weapon will compliment your bard's role as a performer, both on the stage and off? What color should his cape be? Which proficiencies will make him a more effective performer or a more memorable personality? Which spells produce effects in line with your bard's persona? How can these spells be used to build up the reputation of your bard? These are the questions to ask yourself.

Playing a bard can be a lot of fun. Play up the details. Add flavor to the game. Immerse the other players in the fantasy of the game. You should always play heavy on description and mood. For example, it isn't the success or failure of an attack that matters, it's the way in which it is made.

As a player you are succeeding at your job if your fellow role-players know the color of your bard's boots, what kind of weapon he wields, the name of his favorite song (better yet, the words to it), the material components to his most-used spells, the lesser details of his personality, his vocal range, *etc*. If they know your bard as if he were a real person, then you are a true bard role-player.

To establish such a realistic character, you must have a very solid mental image of your bard's appearance, personality, and mannerisms. For believability, these aspects must be predetermined, consistent, and you must portray them reliably.

Some role-players are skilled at establishing such a solidly defined character. Often they base the bard upon a character in a movie or book that they know. Others spend hours mentally developing their bard and getting to know him as a friend. Some generate pages of notes to help them out. You can use any method you like and the following section should help you out with this process.

Defining Your Bard's Personality

Most of the other Complete Handbooks present sample personality types. It can be very useful to read over these sections to help you define your character's personality. Although such descriptions are colorful and useful, they just begin to establish the many facets that you should define for a bard.

Generating complete examples of individual bard personalities would take pages of text and would result in only a dozen options for you to choose from. For this reason, personality types are not presented in this handbook. Rather, the following section contains many traits of a character's personality, along with several examples of each trait.

Although examples under each trait are numbered, you should only roll randomly if you are having a hard time selecting an appropriate trait. Also note that randomly rolling every trait will likely result in combinations that make little sense or are unplayable. So go through and carefully select your character's traits. Keep in mind his kit, alignment, race, other traits, and all other elements that you have already defined.

Note that the examples under each trait are not exhaustive. Feel free to select any other descriptive term that could define the trait. You can also select one or more traits within a specific category if they aren't contradictory. Also, note that the following list of traits is far from complete. Selecting the following traits will help define your bard's persona and is a good start, but you should expand these descriptive terms in your own mind or on paper. Examine your character as a whole, then fill in the gaps and add some extra details.

Personality

Rationality
1. Neurotic
2. Normal
3. Slightly insane
4. Stable
5. Unstable
6. Very stable

Mannerism
1. Careless
2. Curious/ Inquisitive
3. Fanatical/ Obsessive
4. Perceptive
5. Precise/ Exacting
6. Relaxed
7. Retiring
8. Somber
9. Studious
10. Suspicious/ Cautious

Self-Esteem
1. Egoist/ Arrogant
2. Humble
3. Modest
4. Proper
5. Proud/ Haughty
6. Servile/ Obsequious

Philosophy
1. Altruist
2. Benevolent
3. Extroverted
4. Hedonist
5. Introverted
6. Malevolent
7. Optimist
8. Pessimist

Intellect
1. Active
2. Anti-intellectual
3. Average
4. Brilliant
5. Flighty
6. Dull
7. Ponderous
8. Scheming

Bravery
1. Brave
2. Calculating
3. Craven
4. Fearless
5. Foolhardy
6. Normal

Morals
1. Aesthetic
2. Amoral
3. Depraved
4. Immoral
5. Lustful
6. Lusty
7. Normal
8. Perverted
9. Sadistic
10. Virtuous

Piety
1. Average
2. Iconoclastic
3. Impious
4. Irreligious
5. Irreverent
6. Martyr/ Zealot
7. Pious
8. Profane
9. Reverent
10. Saintly

Motivation
1. Driven
2. Energetic
3. Lazy
4. Motivated
5. Normal
6. Slothful

Interests

Hobbies
1. Altruism
2. Athletics
3. Community service
4. Dancing
5. Exotic animals
6. Fishing
7. Foods & Preparation
8. Gambling
9. Handicrafts
10. History
11. Horticulture
12. Hunting
13. Husbandry
14. Legends
15. Nature
16. None
17. Politics
18. Religion
19. Smoking & Pipes
20. Wines & Spirits

Loves
1. Armor
2. Artwork
3. Books & Scrolls
4. Coins & Tokens
5. Knives & Daggers
6. Minerals & Gems
7. Ornaments & Jewelry
8. Porcelain, China & Crystal
9. Shields & Weapons
10. Swords
11. Trophies & Skins
12. Weapons

Fears
1. Caves
2. Enclosed places
3. Crowds
4. Dark
5. Dying
6. Heights
7. Horses
8. Insects
9. Loneliness
10. Pain
11. Poison
12. Priests
13. Sight of own blood
14. Snakes
15. Spiders
16. Torture
17. Traps
18. Undead
19. Water
20. Wizards

Hates
1. Authority
2. Bad food
3. Beggars
4. Braggarts
5. Bullies
6. Greed
7. Guards
8. Heretics
9. Laws
10. Lower class

11	Farmers
12	Priests
13	Rival clan
14	Selfishness
15	Stupidity
16	Thieves
17	Big cities
18	Upper class
19	Warriors
20	Wizards

Relationships

Allies

1	Baker
2	Beggars
3	Blacksmith
4	Constable
5	Foreigner
6	Innkeeper
7	King
8	Local college
9	Mayor
10	Merchant
11	Prince
12	Princess
13	Sage
14	Sheriff
15	Slave master
16	Tavern master
17	Thief
18	Thieves' Guild
19	Warrior
20	Wizard

Foes

1	Beggars
2	Criminals
3	Dragons
4	Dwarves
5	Elves
6	Gnomes
7	Half-elves
8	Half-races
9	Halflings
10	Highwaymen

11	Humans
12	Lizard men
13	Lower class
14	Nonhumans
15	Planar beings
16	Ruffians
17	Thieves
18	Underworlders
19	Upper class
20	Use ally list

Manner

1	Abrasive
2	Antagonistic
3	Blustering
4	Capricious/ Mischievous
5	Compassionate/ Sensitive
6	Courteous
7	Diplomatic
8	Forceful
9	Foul/ Barbaric
10	Helpful/ Kindly
11	Hostile
12	Opinionated/ Contrary
13	Overbearing
14	Practical joker/ Prankster
15	Rash
16	Rude
17	Trusting
18	Vengeful
19	Violent/ War-like
20	Well-spoken

Mood/Disposition

1	Aloof
2	Cheerful
3	Cruel/ Callous
4	Easygoing

5	Even-tempered
6	Forgiving
7	Hard-hearted
8	Harsh
9	Hot-tempered
10	Pleasant
11	Moody
12	Silly
13	Peaceful
14	Reserved
15	Scheming
16	Soft-hearted
17	Solitary/ Secretive
18	Taciturn
19	Unfeeling/ Insensitive
20	Unforgiving

Honesty

1	Average
2	Deceitful
3	Liar
4	Scrupulous
5	Truthful
6	Very honorable

Appearance/ Possessions

General

1	Dandyish
2	Dignified
3	Foppish
4	Imposing
5	Slob
6	Spartan
7	Stately
8	Typical

Quantity

1	Above Average
2	Abundant
3	Average
4	Exceptional
5	Few
6	Scant

Quality

1	Cheap
2	Durable
3	Garish
4	Functional
5	High
6	Junk
7	Kingly
8	Low
9	Practical
10	Trash

Personal Habits

1	Disheveled
2	Immaculate
3	Nonchalant
4	Organized
5	Perfectionist
6	Prim and proper
7	Scatterbrained
8	Sloppy

State of Clothing

1	Clean
2	Dirty
3	Immaculate
4	Ragged
5	Rough
6	Unkempt

Thrift

1	Aesthetic
2	Average
3	Charitable
4	Covetous
5	Generous
6	Greedy
7	Miserly
8	Spendthrift
9	Thrifty
10	Wastrel

Performances

Now that you have your bard fully defined, it is time to put on a show. Bards perform in every situation, from street shows to elaborate performances in the town's grand theater. This section contains the information you and your Dungeon Master need to determine the cost, turnout, and income from such performances.

In several places in this section, a proficiency check is asked for without the exact proficiency being specified. The actual proficiency depends upon the type of performance. If the bard is playing an instrument, use the musical instrument proficiency; if he is juggling knives, use the juggling proficiency; and if he is singing, use the singing proficiency. Thus, the proficiency check matches the performance being given.

Street-side Performances

Street-side performances include any situation in which the bard plays for a changing audience in a public place. Bards can try playing on the sides of streets, in front of public buildings, in the town bazaar, *etc.*

All a bard needs to perform street-side is a coin collection device (a box, cup, or open knapsack), his performing implements, and some time.

In some towns and villages, the law considers street-side performers to be beggars and vagrants. In such towns a permit containing a wax seal set with the appropriate official's ring must be carried or the performer is likely to end up paying twice the amount he made and possibly spending a night in the town dungeon. The typical fee for such a document is 1 gp. The document is good as long as it lasts (which is usually 1d8 days, due to the fragile nature of the wax).

The big danger or thrill (depending upon point of view) of performing street side lies in the performer's exposure. Thieves consider street-side performers to be easy pickings; even beggars have been known to loot a bard's takings. On occasion a gang of ruffians will attack the performer in an attempt to gain his valuables (instruments are well worth such a risk).

Performing street side for money is considered a desperate act; a bard with a reputation of 10 or above loses two places on the ladder during any week in which he gives such a performance.

The income gained from a street-side performance is figured by rolling both a proficiency check and a reputation check. The number of successful rolls (0 [both fail], 1, or 2 [both succeed]) is checked against the conditions, as determined by the Dungeon Master, on Table 29. The bard's total income from the performance is determined by multiplying the hourly income (found in Table 29) by the number of hours the bard performs that day.

New checks are needed for each day's performance.

Table 29: HOURLY STREET-SIDE INCOME

Conditions	Successful Checks		
	0	1	2
Horrid	0	1 cp	1d2 cp
Poor	0	1d2 cp	1d4 cp
Fair	1 cp	1d4 cp	1d8 cp
Good	1d4 cp	1d2 sp	1d4 sp
Excellent	1d10 cp	1d4 sp	1d8 sp
Fabulous	1d4 sp	1d8 sp	1d4 gp

Booked Performances

A booking is an arrangement in which a bard entertains the crowd of some private business (usually a tavern). The tavern master and bard come to some prearranged agreement as to the income, hours, and type of entertainment. The bard (and his assistants if any) simply show up and perform. The tavern master always has a place set aside for the performer. Perhaps a small stage, a corner of the tavern floor, or even some old keyboard instrument.

Typically, it is the bard's responsibility to bring all the instruments required for his performance. Other than that, the bard has no set expenses. Drinks are usually on the house as long as the bard doesn't select the more expensive items. However, it is considered professional to tip the bar maids and wenches heavily when they bring a performer drinks (it sets a good example for the customers).

Few cities have any legal limitations on booked performances.

Although a booked performer is a bit more protected from snatch-and-run thieves, the danger from bar fights and brawls is almost as bad. It is unlikely that the bard will lose money in such situations, but his body and instruments can be severely damaged.

Bookings are considered a good starting place for bards. Such performances satisfy the requirement for a bard to perform locally in a

town in order to maintain his reputation. However, highly reputable bards (13 or higher) suffer a −1 reputation adjustment for giving a booked performance in any but the most lavish surroundings.

The method of payment varies widely from tavern to tavern and from low to high social level. The tendency is for the tavern master to pay the bard a set salary once a night, week, or month. On top of this, wise tavern masters also allow bards to put out a collection bowl. This ensures that the bard gives his all during the performance.

Collection bowls gain money at the street-side performance rate specified on Table 29. The salaried income should be determined randomly on the following table. The bard can then adjust this random result by one in any direction if he rolls a successful reputation check or a proficiency check, or by two if he succeeds with both checks.

Table 30: BOOKED INCOME

D8 Roll	Salary
1	Free room
2	A free meal
3	Room and board
4	Double the collection bowl contents
5	5 electrum per night
6	5 gold per night
7	2d8 gold
8	2d12 gold

Carnivals

The term carnival is used here to include any circus, carnival, caravan, or other traveling form of entertainment. All of these groups arrive at most towns from time to time. During the local harvest season, circuses often arrive to join in the celebration and festivities. Holidays are often targeted by carnival bands. Occasionally the governing body of a large city actually contracts for a carnival as part of a fund raising drive.

Carnival bands are complex and expensive operations to run, and they include multiple performers. It is easiest for a bard to join in an existing carnival, but if he wants to start his own he has to invest some time and money. The base list of needed assets includes at least one wagon (though a one-wagon carnival is unlikely to see much success), horses or oxen to pull it, entertaining implements, portable performance area (a stage, tents, *etc.*), several high-quality performers, and the necessary support crew (teamster, cook, carpenter, *etc.*). Total outlay of gold for such an operation is in the thousands of gold pieces.

It is illegal in most towns and villages for a carnival to simply set up tents and begin performing (unless it is well outside of the town walls). Legal permission ranges from simple verbal approval to purchasing a carnival or circus permit from the town. Such permits typically cost 50 gold per tent, stage, or per-forming area and are generally good for one week.

The dangers a carnival faces are much the same as those faced by a traveling merchant: highway robbery, pirates (during water transport), and monster raids are common. Even within the walls of a town, a carnival is far from safe. Thieves and beggars are attracted to carnivals like flies. Although these lowlifes typically play the crowd, they aren't against making off with a valuable instrument or the carnival strong box. Even more dangerous are the rival carnivals and performers who are in competition for the same audience. Such groups occasionally resort to practical jokes, vandalism, employing bullies, or even hiring assassins to drive off the competition.

Performing in a carnival is considered quite reputable and satisfies the performance criteria of reputation up to and including a reputation of 17. If a more reputable bard performs for any but the most elite carnivals, he will suffer a −1 adjustment to his local reputation.

Carnival performers are given free room and board while on the road (typically some blankets and a mat to throw in, under, or around the wagon or tents at night and relatively good food from the traveling cook). On top of this, they make wages. The normal arrangement is that each performing night's income is divided up as follows: 50% to the carnival master and 50% to the crew. The crew's half of the money is not split evenly. Each member is assigned a number of shares. Typical shares are as follows:

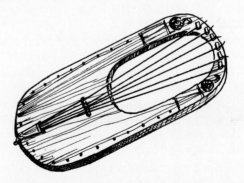

Table 31: CARNIVAL SHARES

Position	Shares of Crew Income
Performers	3 + (# of successful checks)*
Cook	4
Carpenter	3
Teamster	2
Stage Hands	1
Guards	Level (generally 1-4)

*Roll one proficiency check and one reputation check; the number of successful checks is used on this table and on Table 32 as well.

The night's total income is equal to the total number of attendees (attendees plus patrons) times the carnival fee.

Each performer draws in a number of attendees based upon a reputation and proficiency check. (These attendees are in addition to applicable patrons—see page 117 for more about patrons.) The number drawn by each performer should be checked separately (for simplicity, DMs may use the "1" column on Table 32 for all NPC performers). Roll both a proficiency check and a reputation check, then consult the following table to determine how many attendees that performer drew into the carnival. Note that this doesn't mean that this is the number that the performer entertains, as attendees drawn in by other performers wander around and observe all the acts.

The typical fee for a night at the carnival is one electrum piece per person (except infants, who are admitted for free). If this carnival's entrance fee is higher or lower, the Dungeon Master will take this into account when he determines the nightly conditions for the purposes of Table 32 (higher fees effectively improve the conditions, lower fees worsen the conditions).

Table 32: NIGHTLY ATTENDANCE PER PERFORMER

Conditions	Successful Checks		
	0	1	2
Horrid	1d4	2d4	3d4
Poor	1d6	2d6	3d6
Fair	1d8	2d8	3d8
Good	1d10	2d10	3d10
Excellent	1d12	2d12	3d12
Fabulous	1d20	2d20	3d20

Shows and Productions

Shows and productions are the big time for performers. These include any performance that takes place in an established building or place where the audience shows up specifically for the performance and nothing else. Some examples include plays and recitals given at the local theater or opera house, concerts at the local music hall, and productions put on at local bard colleges. Such a performance is either a regularly scheduled event or is accompanied by a lot of promotion and advertising.

The cost of putting on a show or production is large. Costs include advertising, facility rental, stage hands, performer's fees, *etc*. A typical outlay is 1d4 silver pieces times the maximum possible crowd (this is usually equal to the available seating).

Shows and performances are usually outside the domain of city laws. Even if there are fees, the owner of the facility is generally responsible for payment (typically an additional silver piece per audience member).

A nice side benefit to such extravagant performances is the unlikely event of victimization. The only crooks who dare mess with such events are high-ranking master thieves or a fully planned hit by the local thieves' guild, though these are very rare occurrences.

It is considered an honor to perform in shows or productions. This satisfies performance requirements for any reputation level and actually boosts reputations of 10 or less by +1. However, it is rare for any performer below a 10 reputation to be invited to perform at such events. The standard auditions eliminate all but the best performers.

Of all performances, productions provide the greatest for potential income, but they are also the most risky. As with carnivals, the net nightly income is equal to the number of attendees times the admittance fee. Typical admittance fees to productions are 1 gold piece, although really elaborate performances put on in extravagant theaters can range up to a platinum piece or more.

Before the actual number of attendees is determined, the maximum possible number must be found. If the performance is to take place within a building, the maximum equals the building's seating capacity. Otherwise, some reasonable number will have to be settled upon between Dungeon Master and the involved players.

Once the maximum possible crowd is determined, each performer rolls both a reputation check and a proficiency check. Take the total number of successful checks from all performers and divide this by the number of checks that were rolled. This gives a number between 0 and 1, inclusive. Multiply this number by the maximum possible crowd to determine how many people actually show up.

If every performer succeeds at both checks, then the maximum possible crowd shows up. If only half of the checks succeed, then the number of attendees is only half the maximum. If 25% succeed, then 25% show up, *etc*. On top of this, bards have their applicable patrons show up.

Half of the net income (attendance fees minus production costs) goes to the facility's owner and the other half is divided among the performers and stage hands using the carnival's share system.

Bards have many comrades throughout their lives. As they climb the ranks of fame toward a great reputation, they rely heavily upon the various bard colleges. These institutions contain fellow performers great and small. Bards meet those who serve as teachers, critics, peers, and friends within the bard colleges.

A bard who proves to be a good entertainer gains a pool of patrons who go out of their way to attend his performances and occasionally help him out. If a bard survives long enough, he eventually gains devoted followers.

Bard Colleges

Bards often associate with one another, especially those who hold similar views and practice similar forms of entertainment. If such a group becomes established, it is known as a college. Colleges are to bards what guilds are to most other characters. These are places in which skills, philosophies, beliefs, and talents are pooled together. However, colleges are too unique to be given the generic label of "guild."

Membership in most guilds is a permanent matter or at least a long-term one. If a thief joins the local thieves' guild, he is likely going to remain there until something drastic happens. This is not so with bards joining bard colleges.

Bards float from one college to the next. When they are visiting a particular city or village, they look up the local college and partake in its functions. Then when the bard's mood changes, he parts with that college and proceeds on his merry way. Colleges serve as a form of specialty inn—members come and stay for a while, then move on.

From one month to the next, the entire membership of a given college can change. As would be expected, this demands that bard colleges be set up in a very loose format. Most colleges have a set of rules posted in some easily accessible location (often just inside the entryway). These rules are amended, repealed, and redrafted as often as membership turnover causes a shift in philosophy.

The functions of a college are determined by the current members. Most meetings are called on an informal basis; those who show up partake in the discussion, practice, or seminar. Such meetings can evolve into a regular event (for a short while), fragment into smaller groups, or simply end in lieu of more exciting events.

Authority is treated as is everything else—in a very nonchalant way. If the current ranking member of the college is a neutral evil bard, authority is determined by age, power, and underhanded tricks. If a lawful neutral bard is in control, authority is governed strictly by a set of written laws and proceedings. Of course, as one leader departs the college and another comes into power, the rules and methods of determining authority are likely to change. A common saying among bards is, "If you don't like the way a college is run, wait a minute and it'll change."

Common Events

There are numerous events that occur at any college. A few of the most common are performances, practices, debates, dress rehearsals, collecting dues, seminars, discussions, gatherings, and general meetings

Performances are given by one or more bards. These range from vocal solos to dancing duets to an entire cast of actors putting on a play. Some performances are restricted to audiences made up of friends or college members. Others are open to the public and help fund the college. Every decent college has a stage or other performance area, but many performances take place at the local theater or in the village square.

All bards are performers of one sort or another, and no performer can elevate his talents by study alone. Practice literally makes per-

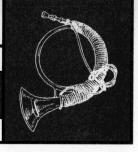

fect for the skills of a bard. Thus numerous practices are held at the college. Here, bards can play before peers, gain the advice of a master, learn the latest techniques for stringing a harp, and so on. If optional training rules are used, college is where most bards train.

Since bards are romantic philosophers at heart, it is no small wonder that debates frequently crop up. Subjects range from the proper way to pluck a mandolin to the best philosophical alignment to hold when going through life. Although debate is defined as a controlled discussion in which two or more sides air their views, it is not uncommon for such debates to boil into heated arguments ending when one side or another draws its weapons and threatens violence.

Before any professional production, a dress rehearsal must take place. This bridges the gap between practices and actual performances. The intent is to run through the entire performance without an audience or only a specially selected audience. This enables the bards to judge the length of the performance and make any last minute alterations. Occasionally, dress rehearsals are used as test performances before a small sample audience. The purpose of this is to determine if the subject matter is too volatile for the target audience.

Dues are usually collected as soon as a bard first enters a college. Typical dues are an electrum piece plus 25% of all income the bard makes while associating with the college (50% if the college is used to put on the performance). If a bard doesn't perform or draws in only small crowds, he will be asked to leave or contribute a platinum piece each week (his decision).

High-level bards often make money at colleges by planning seminars and other events and charging a cover fee (usually a few silver pieces). Seminars are events in which a small panel of bards (usually 1 to 3) presents information on some predetermined topic. Seminars are learning events; those who attend

expect to have fun, learn something useful, and get a chance to ask questions of the masters. Seminar audiences should always be at least two levels below those of the panel. Thus, a bard must be at least 3rd level to put on a seminar.

Discussions are simply planned events in which a small- to medium-sized group (3-10) of bards get together and discuss a topic. The subject can be professional (acting techniques, how to clean instruments), relaxing (reminiscing about the good old days), or philosophical (discussing the lifestyle of the pixie). Discussions are very loose in format, and no one is necessarily in charge.

Gatherings are some of the most cherished events of a college. A gathering is rarely a planned formal event. Rather, it occurs when several bards begin talking about the same topic, such as the proper tempo for an epic poem. In other words, gatherings are acquaintance meetings. Stories are swapped, tales told, rumors shared, and laughs had by all. Occasionally a gathering is planned, such as an early brunch or late evening ball.

Finally, no college would be complete without the general college meeting. These are formal events held for the sole purpose of discussing the college, its policies, future, and other functions. Some college meetings are mandatory; a fine (1 sp) or penalty must be paid by those who do not show. Common topics include assigning personnel to cleaning and cooking details, discussing methods for advertising college performances, voting on whether or not to perform at a local duke's wedding, and so on.

Patrons

As a bard's reputation grows, he begins to attract patrons. These people go out of their way to attend the bard's performances. Some even take up traveling with the bard on short performing tours. Such devoted patrons often serve the bard as stage hands.

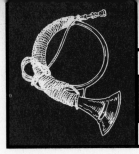

Patrons should not be confused with followers. Patrons are more interested in a bard's performances than in the bard as an individual. They are caught up with the bard's artistic talents. Some will travel miles to attend as many performances as possible, others donate silver and gold to ensure that their favorite performer can support his career. Devoted patrons love his performances so much that they are willing to help him out in order to get him on stage more often. Patrons are a valuable commodity to bards and are always treated with care.

Initial Patrons

Acquiring, gaining, and losing patrons is based upon the optional reputation system presented in this handbook. If this system isn't used, substitute the bard's level for his reputation.

Once a bard becomes well-known (reputation 6) he gains his first patrons. To determine how many patrons the bard initially gains, roll 1d20 a number of times equal to the bard's maximum number of henchmen (a function of Charisma). Every result equal to or below the bard's reputation indicates that one more patron is acquired.

Note that patrons are not henchmen and do not count against this number.

Gaining and Losing Patrons

The number of a bard's patrons fluctuates as the bard's reputation changes. Any time the bard's reputation increases, more patrons can be gained. The bard rolls 1d20 in an attempt to roll equal to or below his new reputation. He can keep rolling until he fails. The number of consecutive rolls equal to or below his new reputation is the number of new patrons

gained. However, the number of a bard's patrons is limited by his maximum number of henchmen and by his level, as shown on Table 33. The number next to the bard's level is multiplied by the bard's maximum number of henchmen (see Table 6 in the *PHB*) to determine the bard's maximum number of patrons.

Table 33: NUMBER OF PATRONS

Bard's Level	Maximum # of Henchmen Times:
1-4	1
5-9	2
10-14	3
15-19	4
20+	5

If a bard's reputation ever drops, he must check to see if any of his patrons leave him. This is done by rolling once for each patron. Any roll above the bard's new reputation indicates that the patron has lost his infatuation with the bard and is no longer a patron. A natural roll of 20 indicates that the patron is very upset with the bard and will have nothing more to do with him.

If you want to add even more detail to your bard's patrons, you can roll on the following table for each one.

Table 34: TYPE OF PATRON

1d20 Roll	Type of Patron	Description
1-10	Fan	Attends every local performance.
11-12	Diehard	Attends every performance within 100 miles and insists on paying 1d4 times what others pay.
13-14	Booster	Attends all local performances and brings 1d6 friends along.
15	Enthusiast	Will serve as a stage hand without charge in exchange for free admittance.
16	Supporter	Roll 1d12; in that many months the supporter will donate 1d10 times the bard's level, in gold, to the bard.
17	Zealot	Zealots follow the bard around to every performance. Some have been known to secretly shadow the bard wherever he goes, even on dangerous quests (from which they seldom return).
18	Defender	Defenders are zealots who have taken it upon themselves to protect the bard, serving as body guards.
19	Extremist	Extremists attempt to mimic the bard as much as possible. They dress like him, act like him, learn his habits, and will even attempt to steal authentic items from him. Some extremists even attempt to befriend the bard's friends and lovers.
20	Fanatic	Fanatics are extremists, but if the bard ever rolls that a fanatic drops from the ranks of his patrons, the fanatic is 25% likely to attempt to assassinate the bard.

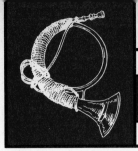

Followers

As stated in the *Player's Handbook*, the True Bard can attract 10d6 0-level soldiers at the 9th level, if he builds a stronghold. These followers arrive over a period of time and are not automatically replaced if lost in battle.

The above information is correct for the True Bard. Of the other kits, only the Skald and some Heralds receive such followers. The other kits receive followers as indicated below.

Table 35: FOLLOWERS BY KIT

Kit	Followers
True	10d6 0-level warriors
Blade	3d6 (use Table 31 in the *PHB*)
Charlatan	1d6 1st-level Charlatans
Gallant	3d4 0-level warriors and 1 3rd-level squire
Gypsy-bard[1]	3d6 gypsies (50% thieves, 20% fighters, 20% fighter/thieves, 5% thief/mages, 4% thief/mages and 1% special [fighter/mage/thief, ranger, bard, druid, bear, *etc.*])
Herald[2]	10d6 0-level warriors **or** 1d4 2nd-level warriors and 1d6 3rd-level thieves
Jester	No followers
Jongleur	3d6 (use Table 31 in the *PHB*)
Loremaster[3]	1d6 1st-level wizards
Meistersinger[4]	Up to 3 animal companions
Riddlemaster	No followers
Skald	10d6 0-level warriors
Thespian[5]	2d12 0-level actors

[1] To attract these followers, a 9th-level (or higher) Gypsy-bard must first purchase a wagon and two carts.

[2] A Herald has two options. If he decides to build a stronghold of his own, he attracts 10d6 0-level warriors. However, if the herald is serving a lord as his agent, the lord donates a section of his fortress to the herald, along with 1d4 2nd-level warriors and 1d6 3rd-level thieves.

[3] Loremasters do not build typical strongholds. Instead, they acquire a tower in the corner of some nobleman's keep, or a house in the scholarly quarter of town.

[4] Meistersingers do not build typical strongholds. They construct a number of hidden cottages instead.

[5] These actors do not have a class and do not gain levels. They pay for all of their own expenses and bring in an additional 1d6 gold each per month for the thespian.

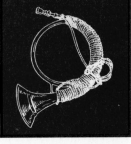

Appendix: 1st Edition Bards

1st Edition Bards Table

Exp. Level	Experience Points	6-Sided Dice for Accum. hp	Level Title	Druid Spells 1 2 3 4 5	College	Addl. Lang. Known	Charm Percentage	Legend Lore and Item Knowledge %
1	0-2,000	0*	Rhymer	1----	(Probationer)	0**	15%	0%
2	2,001-4,000	1	Lyrist	2----	Fochlucan	0	20%	5%
3	4,001-8,000	2	Sonneteer	3----	Fochlucan	0	22%	7%
4	8,001-16,000	3	Skald	31---	Fochlucan	1	24%	10%
5	16,001-25,000	4	Racaraide	32---	MacFuirmidh	0	30%	13%
6	25,001-40,000	5	Jongleur	33---	MacFuirmidh	1	32%	16%
7	40,001-60,000	6	Troubadour	331--	MacFuirmidh	1	34%	20%
8	60,001-85,000	7	Minstrel	332--	Doss	0	40%	25%
9	85,001-110,000	8	Muse	333--	Doss	1	42%	30%
10	110,001-150,000	9	Lorist	3331-	Doss	1	44%	35%
11	150,001-200,000	10	Bard	3332-	Canaith	0	50%	40%
12	200,001-400,000	10 + 1	Master Bard	3333-	Canaith	1	53%	45%
13	400,001-600,000	10 + 2	M. Bard 13th	33331	Canaith	1	56%	50%
14	600,001-800,000	10 + 3	M. Bard 14th	33332	Cli	0	60%	55%
15	800,001-1,000,000	10 + 4	M. Bard 15th	33333	Cli	1	63%	60%
16	1,000,000-1,200,000	10 + 5	M. Bard 16th	43333	Cli	1	66%	65%
17	1,200,001-1,400,000	10 + 6	M. Bard 17th	44333	Anstruth	0	70%	70%
18	1,400,001-1,600,000	10 + 7	M. Bard 18th	44433	Anstruth	1	73%	75%
19	1,600,001-1,800,000	10 + 8	M. Bard 19th	54443	Anstruth	1	76%	80%
20	1,800,001-2,000,000	10 + 9	M. Bard 20th	54444	Ollamh	1	80%	85%
21	2,000,001-2,200,000	10 + 10	M. Bard 21st	55444	Ollamh	1	84%	90%
22	2,200,001-3,000,000	10 + 11	M. Bard 22nd	55544	Ollamh	1	88%	95%
23	3,000,001-up	10 + 12	M. Bard 23rd	55555	Magna Alumnae	1	95%	99%

* The bard has as many Hit Dice as he has previously earned as a fighter (plus the possible addition of those earned as a thief, if that class level exceeds the class level of fighter). All bard Hit Dice (and additional hit points) are additions to existing Hit Dice—none are lost for becoming a bard.

** The character may already know languages from his previous experience.

Notes Regarding the 1st Edition Bards Table

- Experience points are strictly those gained as a bard. All previously earned experience points are not considered here.
- Experience level is that of the bard class only. There is no level beyond the 23rd. The bard gains druidic powers as a druid of the same level would, and he learns and casts spells exactly as a druid of the same level, but he does not progress beyond the 12th level of druid ability until the 23rd level (at which time he casts spells at the 13th level of ability). Bards can read scroll that contain druidic spells.
- At first level, the bard has as many Hit Dice as he has previously earned as a fighter (plus the possible addi-

tion of those earned as a thief if that class exceeds the class level of fighter). All bard Hit Dice (and additional hit points) are additions to existing Hit Dice—none are lost for becoming a bard.
- College is an important distinction to a bard; he will not associate with a bard of a lesser college. The exceptions to this rule are the *Magna Alumnae*, who will happily aid (by advice and suggestion) any bard of any level.
- The bard need not study to learn the additional languages indicated on the table—this process is subsumed as previous work.
- Charm percentage is the chance the bard has of successfully casting a *charm person* (or *charm monster*) spell with his music. It does not negate any immunities or saving throws vs. magic.
- Legend lore and item knowledge percentage shows the

chance a bard has of knowing something about a legendary person, place, or thing, or of knowing what a particular magical item is. The latter ability is limited to weapons, armor, potions, scrolls, and those items of magical nature that the bard can employ or which bear magical inscriptions. All bards know runes, glyphs, characters, symbols, *etc*. Naturally, any knowledge gained by the bard while in his former classes is retained at all levels.

Class Description
As this character class subsumes the functions of two other classes—fighters and thieves—and tops them off with magical abilities, it is often not allowed by Dungeon Masters. Even though this presentation is greatly modified from the original bard class, it is offered as supplemental to the system, and the DM will be the final arbiter as to the inclusion of bards in the campaign.

A bard must have scores of 15 or better in the following abilities: Strength, Wisdom, Dexterity, and Charisma. He must also have an Intelligence score of at least 12 and a Constitution score of at least 10. The character must be either a human or a half-elf.

Bards begin play as fighters and must remain exclusively so until they have achieved at least the 5th level of experience. Anytime thereafter, and in any event prior to attaining the 8th level, they must change to the thief class. Sometime between 5th and 9th level, bards must leave the thief class and become a druid—at this time, they are actually bards under druidic tutelage. Bards must fulfill the requirements in *all* the above classes before progressing to the (1st Edition) **Bards Table**. They must always remain Neutral, but they may be Good, Chaotic, Good, or Lawful if they wish.

A bard always engages in combat at the level he attained as a fighter. Likewise, he is able to function as a thief of the level attained. All saving throws are made on the most favorable table, with the actual bard level considered to be that of a druid. He must always have a stringed instrument.

The bard's poetic ability raises the morale of associated creatures by 10%. It likewise can inspire ferocity in battle, so attack rolls gain a +1 bonus. Both effects require two rounds to inspire the desired effect, and they last for one turn. Note that the bard can engage in combat while engaged in this ability, but he cannot sing or cast spells.

A bard's singing and playing negates the song effects of harpies and similar attacks that rely upon song. It negates the sound of shriekers, who are soothed by the sound of the bard's instrument.

When the bard plays his instrument, creatures (not in the bard's party) within 4" of the bard must roll successful saving throws vs. spell or sit entranced while the bard performs. Even those creatures who are not charmed by the bard will still stop and listen for one round. Charmed creatures are subject to a suggestion (as the spell), and if the bard implants the suggestion in his song, the charmed creatures must roll a successful saving throw vs. spell with a −2 penalty or be subject to the full impact of the suggestion. Those who save are totally free of the bard's *charm* effect. Each creature is susceptible to this ability once per day. Loud noise or physical attack will negate the charm, but not the suggestion.

Due to his training, a bard has knowledge of many legendary and magical items after the 1st level of experience, and this knowledge improves with advancement. If some legendary knowledge is appropriate and the dice score indicates that the bard has knowledge in that area, then his ability will deliver information similar to the magic-user spell, *legend lore*. Without actually touching an item, the bard also has a like chance of determining its magical properties and alignment. This latter ability is limited to armor, miscellaneous weapons, miscellaneous magical items (if usable by a druid, fighter, or thief—unless inscribed with magical writing, in which case the bard can read what is written at the least), potions, rings, rods *et al.* (if usable by a druid, fighter, or thief), and scrolls. Artifacts and relics are not considered "miscellaneous magical items."

Bards are able to use magical items that are permitted to druids, fighters, and thieves. Magical books/librams/tomes that pertain to the same are also beneficial (or baneful) to bards, and these items can raise fighting or thieving abilities beyond the norm. (If a writing is baneful, treat the bard as the least favorable of his classes.) Miscellaneous magical items of a musical nature are superior when employed by a bard, such as *drums of panic* (−1 to saving throws), a *horn of blasting* (50% greater damage), a *lyre of building* (the effects are doubled), and *pipes of the sewer* (twice the number of rats in half the usual time).

Bards may wear leather or magical chain mail only and may not use shields. They may use any type of club, dagger, dart, javelin, sling, scimitar, spear, or staff. They may also use a bastard, long, or short sword. They may employ oil, but never poison (unless they are Neutral Evil in alignment).

Bards will never serve as a henchman for longer than one to four months. They are unable to employ henchmen other than druids, fighters, or thieves of human, half-elf, or elf stock. It is possible for a bard to attract one henchman upon attaining 5th level, two at 8th level, three at 11th level, four at 14th level, five at 17th level, six at 20th level, and any number of them at 23rd level (subject to the bard's Charisma). Only bards of 23rd level may settle down and construct a stronghold of any sort.

Note: If bards are permitted in your campaign, there is a possibility that the DM will also include certain magical items that are usable only by bards.

Bard Character Record Sheet

Player _____ Character _____

Date Created _____ Kit Name _____

Race _____ Alignment _____

Ability Scores

☐ STR	Max Press _____ lbs. Open Doors _____ (_____) in 20 Bend Bars/Lift Gates _____ %
☐ DEX	Surprise: 1-3 in 10 _____
☐ CON	System Shock _____ %
☐ INT	(Missing entries go in other areas of this record sheet.)
☐ WIS	
☐ CHA	Max # Henchmen _____ Loyalty Base _____ Reaction Adjustment _____

Experience

☐ 10% Bonus if 16 Dex and Con

Level ☐

Limit ☐

Individual XP	#	Worth	
Thief Skills		100	200
Written Magic		200	200
Special Benefits		150	200
Spell Levels		25	—
Entertain		100	—
Performance		500	—
Gold		1	2
Hit Die Defeated		■ 5	■ 5
Other		PHBR or DMG	

TOTAL _____

Next Level _____

Saving Throws

Start	*	Total	
13	−1		Paralyzation/Poison/Death
14	−2		Rod/Staff/Wand
12	−1		Petrification/Polymorph
16	−1		Breath Weapon
15	−2		Spell

* = change at 5th, 9th, 13th, 17th, 21st, etc., levels

+/−	Condition	+/−	Condition

Hit Points

Current _____

Total _____

1st-10th level = 1d6 + _____

11th on = +2 only _____ (Con.)

■ Regenerate _____

DEATH: Max # ☐ Initial (Con. + 1)

To date _____

Resurrection Survival _____

Armor Class

AC ☐

Worn _____

△ Base

+/−	Condition	+/−	Condition

Level Changes

THAC0	Odd levels
HP	All
Saves	5,9,13,17,21
Proficiencies	4,8,12,16,20
Thief Skills	All
Spells	All
Reputation	Check at all
Followers	9th
Use Written	10th

Target's AC	10	9	8	7	6	5	4	3	2	1	0	−1	−2	−3	−4	−5	−6	−7	−8	−9	−10
Attack Number																					
Weapon Slots	☐ = 2 + (1 at 4, 8, 12, 16, 20, etc.)									THAC0	= 20 (−1 every odd level past 1st)										

Combat

Weapons	Attack Adj.				#AT	Damage						Shots Fired		
	Usual	0	−2	−5	ROF	S/M	L	Sp	Ty	Sz	Type	#	Used
			—Range—										

Attack / Both / Damage

+/−	Attack Condition	+/−	Both Condition	+/−	Damage Condition

Notes

Bard Character Record Sheet

Nonweapon Proficiencies

Slots ☐ = _____ +3 (+1 at 4, 8, 12, 16, 20, etc.)
          (Int.)

Notes

Proficiency		Req.	Ability Score +/−	Mod.	Add'l + Slots	=	Total
B O N U S							

S U G G E S T E D & O T H E R							

■ Secondary Skill:

Thief Skills

Base	Skill*	Race	Dex	Kit	Armor	Total		Notes
10						%	Pick Pockets	Mountaineering = +10% per slot
20						%	Detect Noise	Bonus Armor
50						%	Climb Walls	
5						%	Read Lang.	*Skill: 1st = +20%, 2nd and on = +15%

■ Use any written magical item with a 15% malfunction chance

Spells   ■ Verbal Component _____

Max. Spell Level _____   Chance to Learn _____ %   Max. #/Level _____

1st _____   2nd _____   3rd _____   4th _____   5th _____   6th _____   7th _____

Racial Abilities

Special Benefits

#1 _____   _____

#2 _____   _____

#3 _____   _____

#4 _____   _____

Kit Notes

Bard Character Record Sheet

Age

Natural + Unnatural = Total

Date Born ___/___/___

Middle		−1 Str & Con; +1 Int & Wis
Old		−2 Str & Dex; −1 Con; +1 Wis
Venerable		−1 Str & Dex & Con; +1 Int & Wis

Maximum Age ____

Vital Statistics

Sex ☐ M ☐ F

Height _____ ' _____ "

Weight _____ lbs.

Hair _____

Eyes _____

Skin _____

Personality Traits

_____
_____
_____
_____
_____
_____
_____

Reputation ▌

Index ____ Title _____

Last Performance ___/___/___

Earnings _____ Spent on Reputation _____

Established Reputations

Index	Town/City

Patrons (gained at Rep. 6)

Current # ____   Maximum ____

Fans	1-10		attend local
Diehards	11-12		attend 100 miles
Boosters	13-14		local + 1d6 friends
Enthusiasts	15		free work
Supporters	16		level x 1d10 gp/1d12 months
Zealots	17		follow
Defenders	18		follow & defend
Extremists	19		mimic
Fanatics	20		mimic (25% kill)

■ Followers (Gained at 9th Level) #: _____ Type: _____

Notes

Equipment Carried

	Left Side				Front/Back				Right Side	
Used/#	Item/Location	unit cost/wt.		Used/#	Item/Location	unit cost/wt.		Used/#	Item/Location	unit cost/wt.

cp	1/100*
sp	1/10*
ep	1/2*
gp	1*
pp	5*

*10 of these = 1 lb.

Debts _____

Will _____

Vision ■ Infravision _____ ft.

Light Source	Radius	Duration	Used

Movement Rate

Base ■ 12 ■ 6

Encumbrance	lbs. Carried	MV	✔	Penalty Attack	AC
Unenc.	—			—	—
Light (⅔ MV)	—			—	—
Mod. (½ MV)	—			−1	—
Heavy (⅓ MV)	—			−2	+1
Severe (1)	1			−4	+3

Bard Kit Record Sheet

Player _____ _____ Character

Kit [_____] DM _____ Campaign _____

Qualifications

Ability Scores

DEX (12*) [___]
INT (13) [___]
CHA (15*) [___]
[___]

_____
Other
* = Prime Requisite   Minimum

Races _____
_____

Alignments _____
_____
_____

Thief Skill Adjustments

Pick Pockets [___]
Detect Noise [___]
Climb Walls [___]
Read Languages [___]
_____
Other   = / −

Description** _____
_____
_____

Role** _____
_____

Secondary Skills
_____
_____
_____
_____
_____

Weapon Proficiencies
_____ _____
_____ _____
_____ _____
_____ _____
_____ _____

Nonweapon Proficiencies

B O N U S   S U G G E S T E D

1 _____   2 _____
3 _____   4 _____
_____ _____
_____ _____
_____ _____
_____ _____
_____ _____

Armor Equipment _____
_____
_____

Special Benefits*

Other
#1 _____ _____
#2 _____ _____
#3 _____ _____
#4 _____ _____
Special Hindrances* _____
_____

Notes* _____
_____

** = These categories should be fully detailed on another sheet of paper.

Index

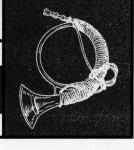